Black Youth

Critical Youth Studies

Series Editor: Greg Dimitriadis

Black Youth Matters

Transitions from School to Success

Cecile Wright, Penny Standen and Tina Patel

Routledge
Taylor & Francis Group

NEW YORK AND LONDON

First published 2010
by Routledge
270 Madison Avenue, New York, NY 10016

Simultaneously published in the UK
by Routledge
2 Park Square, Milton Park, Abingdon, Oxon OX14 4RN

Routledge is an imprint of the Taylor & Francis Group, an informa business

Typeset in Caslon by RefineCatch Limited, Bungay, Suffolk
Printed and bound in the United States of America on acid-free paper by
Walsworth Publishing Company, Marceline, MO

Library of Congress Cataloging in Publication Data
Wright, Cecile.
Black youth matters : transitions from school to success / Cecile Wright, Penny
    Standen, Tina Patel.
      p. cm. – (Critical youth studies)
    Includes bibliographical references and index.
    1. Discrimination in education – Great Britain.   2. Youth, Black – Education –
    Great Britain.   3. Youth, Black – Great Britain – Social conditions.   4. Success –
    Great Britain.   I. Standen, Penny.   II. Patel, Tina G.   III. Title.
    LC212.3.G7W74 2009
    379.2'6—dc22
                              2009025385

ISBN 10: 0–415–99510–8 (hbk)
ISBN 10: 0–415–99512–4 (pbk)
ISBN 10: 0–203–86305–4 (ebk)

ISBN 13: 978–0–415–99510–8 (hbk)
ISBN 13: 978–0–415–99512–2 (pbk)
ISBN 13: 978–0–203–86305–3 (ebk)

Contents

Series Editor Introduction

GREG DIMITRIADIS

Black Youth Matters: Transitions from School to Success is an important and timely volume. Collectively, Cecile Wright, Penny Standen, and Tina Patel present a compelling, empirical picture of black youth creatively responding to permanent school exclusion in the UK. As the authors demonstrate, these young people are "framed" by the school as failures in very explicit and demonstrable ways. This notion of failure is picked up and codified by work on stratification in the UK that traces the limited class mobility of black youth. While useful in many ways, this work has served to delimit notions of youth "success" and the different ways young people can—and do—transition to adulthood. Importantly, the authors highlight how black youth can draw on community resources as well as broader diasporic histories and collective identities in forging alternative notions of success.

The move is an important one. As the authors demonstrate, literature on social and economic mobility has tended to be framed by particular notions of "cultural capital." Drawing on the work of Bourdieu and Passeron (1977), critical scholars have looked to map the ways youth are able or not able to mobilize and translate particular kinds of cultural and economic "capital" to move across class lines. This literature has largely, the authors argue, written out the experiences of black youth. As the authors show, young people who face school exclusion often draw on other kinds of capital—in particular "aspirational capital"—to achieve other kinds of success (Yosso, 2005). Excavating these concerns is this volume's great triumph.

Indeed, through a two-year ethnographic study, the authors show how young people respond to school exclusion with a sense of possibility—not despair. These young people often see their struggles in school as key, "critical moments" that they use to envision and re-envision different kinds of futures for themselves. Importantly, these youth do not do so on their own. Rather, they turn to family, peers, friends, and other kinds of community networks to help imagine other kinds of successes for themselves. These young people demonstrate a kind of resilience that can only be understood in the broader context of race in the UK. The authors show how neither sociological nor psychological explanations alone can exhaust the complexities of black youth experiences here. Wright, Standen, and Patel work towards a new language around social mobility, one that accounts for the hard work black youth do in transforming exclusion into new kinds of aspiration and success.

In so doing, the authors pose a key challenge to the kinds of narrow narratives that have long framed black youth. For the authors, race is a resource these young people draw on individually and collectively to transform painful experiences into small and large triumphs. By opening up this notion of "capital," the authors give us a new angle of vision on the question of race and how it is lived today. The authors point to both the enduring inequalities that black youth live with today as well as the resources that can be generated from such struggle. Yet, the authors do not give us only isolated narratives—success stories, so to speak. They look at the broader patters at work here, the collective sedimentation of such aspirational capital and how it is generated with and embedded in broader black communities. The authors give us a more systematic language to think through questions of educational exclusion and race.

This, too, is an intellectual triumph. While structural approaches to social stratification often set the terms of discussion around racial inequality and success—often posing remedies that place youth

squarely in deficiency spaces—the authors intervene with an alternative but complementary language. They both engage with and move
beyond structural models of stratification and education, affirming the
enduring importance of individual and collective aspiration—an
impulse that has not been exhausted for black youth even in the face
of systematic, longstanding, and overwhelming inequality.

References

Bourdieu, P. & Passeron, J.-C. (1977). *Reproduction in education, society and culture*. Thousand Oaks: Sage.
Yosso, T. J. (2005). Whose culture has capital? A critical race theory discussion of community cultural wealth. *Race, Ethnicity and Education*, *8*, (1), 69–91.

Acknowledgements

The research reported was funded by the Joseph Rowntree Foundation.

We wish to thank the researchers who have been involved in this study: Dr Caroline Howarth, Sonia Davis, Dr Annecka Marshall, George Fisher and Levi Heban. We would like to thank Christine Callender, Sonia Thompson, Vanessa Augusta, P. C. Gilbert, Tony Graham, Paul Grant, Anne Downie, Councillor Des Wilson, Courtney Rose, Philip Hayes, Linda Wright, Steve Small, Kevin Brown (formerly of Build), Michael Henry, Steve Philips, Cleveland Thompson, Henry Kevin Brown (Senior Youth Worker), Lee Jasper, Lee Parker, Rev. Hughie La Rose, Sue Wheeldon, Yvonne Aubrey, Kate Dickson, Declan Gaffney, Diane Abbott, Maud Blair, Ann Phoenix, Veronica Price-Job, Balbir Chatrik, Owen and Charlie Lloyd. We also thank Sandra Odell for providing vital administrative support throughout the period of the research and Terry Hanstock, librarian at Nottingham Trent, for providing essential support throughout the period of the production of this book.

Thanks too must go to the young people and their families and carers and the many agencies involved – without their willingness to give so generously of their time and information this study would not have been possible. To our families and all those from whom we have drawn social and cultural capital!

INTRODUCTION

This book is about young black people's educational experience and how they work to transform school 'failure'. It is set in the United Kingdom (UK) and is concerned with how young people manage, survive and recovered from this earlier school 'failure' after monumental personal effort. We describe and examine the resourcefulness of young black people in forging their futures and how the notion of 'aspirational capital' (Yosso, 2005) promotes resilience and a 'culture of possibility'. The role of community organisations, family, kinship and friends are explored in overcoming the process of 'school failure'. The particular representation of black young people referred to throughout the book relates to young people of African descent throughout the diaspora. In the UK African-Caribbean people, that is people of African-Caribbean origin or descent and family heritage, are the third largest and most instantly recognisable migrant community in the UK (Owen, 1977; Goulbourne, 2002). Similarly, within the US the term is usually taken to denote people of African-American ethnic heritage.

This book emerges out of a longitudinal study in which our research was documented over a two-year period. The study combined quantitative data with qualitative interviewing. The data upon which the book is based include 100 narrative interviews conducted with 33 young people: 21 male, 12 female between the ages of 14 and 19 who had experienced permanent school exclusion.[1] The young people were drawn from those resident in Nottingham and London who had been excluded from both state and independent schools. The young people were interviewed on a maximum of three occasions over the period of two years. Participants were asked to talk about various aspects of three themes: their view of self following exclusion, sources of support and coping strategies for transforming school exclusion and their views of current personal circumstances and ambitions for the future. Additional data are provided from over 60 interviews with contacts nominated by the young people including community and social workers, mothers, fathers, grandparents, siblings and friends.

Traditionally these young people are often described as hard to reach (Merton, 1998). Thus a snowballing sample method was used to access the young people for the study. These included contacts with African-Caribbean community groups, black organisations, supplementary schools and the black church. The nature of this snowballing process meant that it was impossible to secure an equal number of young people in terms of gender and age. Meetings with the young people were conducted in varied locations including their homes, the university and community venues.

Integral to the research design was the desire to both engage and empower the young people. In this vein the use of visual methods was valuable in the following respects. First, we anticipated that traditional one-to-one interviewing would not necessarily be the best way to carry out the research with the young excluded people because they are likely to have experienced many interview situations where the aim was to prove their responsibility for the exclusion. After considering other methods, visual research methods, namely participant photography, was chosen to place young people at the centre of the research process. The aim was to provide them with the opportunity to discuss and visually represent their lives from their experiences. To achieve this, disposable cameras were given to the participants. They were asked to take pictures over the course of three months of family, friends and anyone else who has been a source of support and people they enjoyed being with. However, they were not told what to photograph, thereby leaving both the content and process to the young person to decide. Photo elicitation interviews were then conducted with all of the young people, drawing on the photographs they had produced and developed. The interviews often contained one or two of the participants. Although an interview with two respondents simultaneously could have inhibited responses, participants were only interviewed together if they had chosen to be photographed together and explained to the researcher that these photographs were symbolic of the support they had provided each other during their exclusion.

Second, one of the obstacles the use of photographs aimed to overcome was the literacy ability of the participants and the often inarticulate experience of the initial interviews. A key consideration that had not been fully anticipated when proposing the research was attempting to engage them in discourse. We became aware of the quandary posed by research aiming to give a voice to an under-represented group of people. What if they do not have the capacity or willingness to articulate themselves? After engaging with them in training sessions and also informally, it became more a question of: what if they need something different to assist them in articulating themselves? Other researchers have also found that poor literacy skills or language problems are a common feature of research with similar cohorts, which can create difficulties (Ovenden and Loxley, 1993; Allen, 2002). This was not the case as the young people fully engaged and articulated their experiences. However, the majority of young people participating in the programmes did have low levels of confidence and self-esteem. It took a significant amount of time to develop a relationship with them to ensure that they were comfortable talking to the researcher. Nevertheless, all the participants were particularly enthusiastic and receptive to the use of cameras. They expressed feelings of empowerment. For them, control over the cameras and the photographs produced gave considerable recognition to the importance of their experiences and perspectives of exclusion.

However, as the empowerment of the research participants was at the core of the research design, further discussion of the efficacy of the status of the researcher within the research process is required. This form of reflexive thinking accords with black feminist researchers' concerns with understanding the intersection of 'race', class, gender and age in the research process (hooks, 1989; Collins, 1990; Apple, 2004; King, 2005; Reynolds, 2005). Our experiences as black female, middle-class researchers interviewing young black females and males, in essence our 'insider/outsider' status, meant that we were attentive to how gender, 'race', class and age status impacts on the research process and interactions with the young people. For instance, whereas our racial and gender ascription minimised our outsider status in our

interaction with the young women, our age and assumed class affili-
ation may have been taken as sources of potential domination. As a
result of our occupations, during the interviews we were perceived
to be middle class because it was felt by the young people that we had
access to certain information and resources that they were restricted
from accessing. Some of the working class young people sought our
opinion about social and educational aspects of further and higher
education. They would also ask for advice on career matters!

The remainder of this introductory chapter will provide a brief
overview of the key set of arguments to be elaborated in the book and
then connect them to the structure and content of the book.

The Context

The focus of our book brings into view wider issues about social
mobility which is a debate that is current in both the UK and the
United States (US) (e.g. Loury et al, 2005; Nunn et al, 2007). Within
this context education is considered to be one of the most important
factors in facilitating and inhibiting social mobility. Both within the
US and the UK the presence of young black people within the respect-
ive education systems has been framed within a discourse of problematic students because of their perceived alien demands and identities
(Archer and Francis, 2007). The *Brown v Board of Education* (1954)
Supreme Court decision emanated from a series of legal challenges
mounted by black families demanding equality of opportunity for
their children. It led the way to school desegregation in the United
States and has been a topic of extensive academic and political debate
(see for example Zirkel and Cantor, 2004). Similarly, because they
believed that black children were assumed to be detrimental to and a
burden on, white schools some educational authorities bussed black
children to different areas in order to spread and minimise the impact
across schools. It was hoped that such dispersal would encourage
(force) the children to 'assimilate' and adapt to the dominant white
culture (Mullard, 1985, p. 1 referred to in Archer and Francis, 2007).
In contrast, in Britain the schooling of black and white young people
was not formally segregated to the same degree, although research
and reports have documented the extent to which black young people

experienced covert segregation through being systematically discriminated against within mainstream British education over the years (see for example the Swann Report, Department of Education and Science, 1985; Mullard, 1985; Eggleston et al, 1986). Crucially, we are also aware that the dominant themes in the discourse relating to young black diasporic people's presence in western education systems and at the point of transition from compulsory education are those of difference, inequality, underachievement and division. In this respect, one of the most commonly discussed issues in American education is the achievement gap which specifically implies the difference in measures of academic proficiency and outcome for example, graduation rates, between African-American/black and white students (Ladson-Billings, 2006). Similarly, in the United Kingdom young people of African-Caribbean heritage feature persistently in low educational achievement and high rates of exclusion from school.

Some Issues: Educational Inequality, Social Exclusion and Young Black People in the UK

Before we outline the main contours of the educational experiences of young black people in the compulsory British education system,[2] it is worth commenting on how the issue of black students and their achievement are framed and understood within UK education research and policy discourse. Historically, studies of black students' educational experiences within the UK, to a great extent, have centred on exploring 'underachievement'. This term has been much contested within the area of 'race' and education which has resulted in a focus on a differentiated pattern in scores on Standard Assessment Tests (SATs),[3] the failure of acquiring particular qualifications or failing to achieve a university place. For instance Wright (1987) argues that the term 'underachievement' has come to be interpreted as signifying widespread failure among young black people, the corollary being that all black students are destined to fail. Wright (1987) argues that the educational experiences of black students are best explained by the concept of educational disadvantage or inequality rather than cultural deficits. Similarly, Troyna (1984) argues that the term superficially shifts responsibility away from the education system to students and their families, rather than focusing on the system's failure to meet the needs of black learners. For this reason, many recent commentators and writers in the area of 'race' and education have preferred to speak of inequality of achievement or opportunity in black students' experience of compulsory education. This signals that their experiences are more a case of injustice rather than unavoidable variation in performance (see for example Gillborn and Gipps, 1996; Archer and Francis, 2007). Hence, the terminology used in this field is of concern not merely in terms of whether the term 'inequality' should be used rather than 'underachievement' but because use of this term is embedded in a conceptualisation that leads us to focus on inequalities in education and measures for ameliorating them. Indeed, as Archer and Francis (2007) note, policy discourses are inflected with notions of underachievement insofar as there has been a tendency to either play down 'race' inequalities in achievement or situate differentiated patterns in school achievement within black students and their families. In this vein, it could be argued that educational policy and practice are connected to hegemonic domination in wider society (Gramsci, 1971) or as Gillborn (2008) argues they constitute 'a form of locked-in inequality that is inevitable and permanent under current circumstances' (p. 45). Also, as Casey observes:

> In a racist society for a black child to become educated is to contradict the whole system of racist signification . . . to succeed in studying white knowledge is to undo the system itself . . . to refute its reproduction of black inferiority materially and symbolically. (Casey, 1993, p. 123)

Since the 1970s there has been an extensive body of research, commentary and public concern about the inequality experienced by black students within the British education system. Moreover, commentaries have attempted to draw out some of the complexities that characterise the patterns of black students' educational attainment. Research indicates that while black children tend to start off their schooling with high ability and show themselves to be capable students, as they get older, their achievements deteriorate (see for example Coard, 1971; Wright, 1987; Christian, 2005; Archer and Francis, 2007; Rhamie, 2007). This is further supported by research that indicates that at primary school the achievement of black children is often higher at

Key Stage 1 than other groups but attainment declines in relation to other groups so that at Key Stage 4 (age 16)[4] it is among the lowest (Wright et al, 2005; Archer and Francis, 2007; Gillborn, 2008). In this respect, it would appear that for black students the gap between their achievement and that of other groups actually broadens rather than narrows as children progress through compulsory education. It has been argued that in illuminating the patterns in comparative achievement across various ethnic groups within the British education system, there is a need also to acknowledge the impact of other social identity variables, namely, gender and social class or socio-economic status. Regarding gender, research reveals that black girls tend to outperform black boys and that a significant proportion of boys compared with girls complete compulsory school with few or no qualifications (Archer and Francis, 2007; Rhamie, 2007). In terms of social class, interestingly, although data show that social class or socio-economic status is a more salient predictor of achievement for the majority of white students, this appears not to be the case for black students. Hence, in Britain it would appear that ethnicity or 'race' are greater predictors of educational achievement than either gender or social class (Bhattacharyya et al, 2003). As Archer and Francis (2007) argue, that the 'ethnicity gap expands rather than narrows for some groups during schooling is a particular indictment of a failure of the British education system to address these pupils' needs and ensure fairness for all' (p. 13). Various writers have considered 'race' and racism to be the central organising principle affecting the performance of black students in schools (Gillborn and Mirza, 2000; Wright et al, 2000; Majors, 2001; Archer and Francis, 2007; Rhamie, 2007; Gillborn, 2008). It is argued that this situation leads to a labelling effect resulting in an increased likelihood of exclusion from the learning process (Christian, 2005).

It is important to recognise that the patterns of low school attainment amongst black students may represent only a partial picture of their experience of schooling. Of frequent concern is the disproportionately high rate of exclusions among black students. Thus, by the time their compulsory schooling is completed a disproportionate number of black students are no longer in school and, in marked contrast to the US where students choose to absent themselves from school or drop out, in Britain the exclusion statistics represent a situation where schools decide they will no longer accept students on their rolls. For black boys, research reveals that they are between four and 15 times more likely to be excluded than white boys, depending on the locality (Sewell, 1997; Department for Education and Employment, 2000a, 2000b) and black girls are four times more likely to be permanently excluded than white girls (Wright et al, 2005). A Department for Education and Skills commissioned study sets the rate of permanent exclusion for black students within an average secondary school at 2.6 times more than that for other students (Parsons et al, 2004). Figures for 2004/5 show 0.3% of black students were permanently excluded from secondary school compared to 0.13% of white students (Department for Education and Skills, 2006). While there are different ways of measuring exclusion, it is clear that inequalities persist in this particular area. Interestingly, the research also reveals that black students involved in school exclusion tend to be of average or above average ability, have not usually exhibited disruptive behaviour prior to attending secondary school and are not usually disaffected with education (Majors, 2001). Official statistics suggest that more than four times as many young people excluded from school fail to gain any qualifications at age 16 when compulsory schooling ends, compared with students not excluded (Social Exclusion Unit, 1999b). In this respect, the disproportionate exclusion of black young people from school has served to illustrate the inequality faced by black students within the British education as being at its most pernicious. Here, student exclusion from school, particularly black student exclusion, is an extremely urgent issue, as Britain's official exclusion figures far outstrip those of other countries in Europe and North America. However, in the US exclusion and suspension figures indicate that high numbers of black students, particularly males, are being suspended or excluded, often for relatively minor incidents and at a much higher rate than their white counterparts (see, for example, Gardner et al, 2001). A related topic of discussion and debate is the negative consequences related to school suspension and exclusion namely, school failure, school dropout, retention and school disengagement (Eitle, 2004). This racial-ethnic and gendered disparity in disciplinary practices has also become an integral part of the debate and discussion relating to closing the achievement gap (e.g. Bay Area School Reform Collaborative, 2003).

The data concerning the nature of black students' schooling inequality or achievement gaps on both sides of the Atlantic are vital and have, indeed, not only produced some useful insights but have undoubtedly shaped developments in policy, funding and practice. For example, within the US context the 'No Child Left Behind Act 2001' (Ladson-Billings, 2006) dictated that states publish achievement results separately by racial group. Closing the reported achievement gap has been included in the second objective of the U.S. Department of Education's Strategic Plan: 2002–2007 (U.S. Department of Education, 2002). By contrast in the UK, it is argued that in the policy domain in recent years there has been a tendency to play down 'race' inequalities in school achievement in spite of their clear and evident persistence. As Gillborn (2005) notes this approach within British education policy reflects 'tacit intentionality' on the part of the Government to ignore or tolerate the situation of black students' inequality and disadvantage in schooling. Rather than rehearing the argument here, please see Majors (2001), Wright et al (2005), Archer and Francis (2007) and Gillborn (2008). In this regard, black students' low attainment within the education system has tended to be addressed through targeted initiatives or programmes, for example the Black Pupils Achievement Programme and EMAG programmes (Cork, 2005; Rhamie, 2007). In both the US and the UK it is argued that the impact of poor educational achievement associated with some young black people, particularly young men, can increase the risk of marginalisation, the longer-term processes of social exclusion and entry into the criminal justice system (Social Exclusion Unit, 1999a; Barn, 2001; Bowling and Phillips, 2002; Wright et al, 2005; Ginwright, 2007).[5] This focus, however, has tended to mean that other potentially important areas of inquiry and debate have been neglected. Further, within the context of the US, Ginwright (2007) posits:

In recent years, social science about Black youth has almost entirely focused on understanding various causes of problems, such as violence, school failure, substance abuse, crime [Anderson, 1990; Anderson, 1999; Anyon, 1997; Norguera, 1995; Wilson, 1987]. Although an understanding of these social problems is indeed important, the narrow focus on problems obscures the complex ways in which Black youth respond

to challenge, and change conditions in their schools and communities.
(p. 404)

We shall explore in the next section the emergence of literature in
both the US and the UK young black people's educational success
or how they work to transform school 'failure'.

Beyond School 'Failure'

This book seeks to move beyond discussion of the school 'failure'
associated with black students in Britain and the achievement gaps
experienced by black students in the US whilst not shirking some
of the critical work in this area. Rather, it takes the view as Rhamie
(2007) points out that it is important to explore all aspects of black
students' experiences within the education system, not only the pattern
of differentiated attainment 'but also the factors that fracture that
pattern and enable academic success' (p. 4). It has become increasingly
evident that questions of black students' educational success merit
consideration for two key aspects. First, focusing on the relative educational success of some young black people is not only important in
its own right but ultimately can provide an opportunity for the recognition and celebration of success. In essence, this would counteract the
negative representations, images and associations of young people as
problems and failures and be a means of highlighting previously hidden
and ignored injustices experienced by successful young black people.
Second, in particular, focusing on young black people who are able
to transform school 'failure' and achieve success can provide greater
insights into educational inequality (Perry, 2003; Archer and Francis,
2007). Indeed, Gibson (1988) asserts from the US context that
'many . . . theories have originated in an effort to explain minority
failure and have been generated without sufficient attention to cases
of minority success' (Gibson, 1988, p. 168). Fordham (1996) in her
book *Blacked out: Dilemmas of race, identity, and success at Capital High*
offers one of the few detailed studies from the US of young black
people's success within the school setting. Interestingly, the study
highlighted that the 'trade-off' for academic success among African-
American adolescents was the relinquishing of elements of their black

culture or having to 'act white' with the subsequent psychological costs (p. 237). Within the UK the few studies which have engaged with the issue of minority educational success in the context of the school have tended to focus on the experiences of high achieving young people of Asian, particularly of Indian or Chinese, origins (see for example Gillborn and Mirza, 2000; Archer and Francis, 2007; Gillborn, 2008). With a few exceptions (Channer, 1995; Rhamie, 2007) evidence of young black people's educational success in the UK has tended to focus on their post-compulsory school experience. Much academic work suggests that, despite their well documented negative experience of the schooling system, young black people are now entering universities at rates higher than their white peers and that they appear to be achieving from a situation of relative disadvantage (Shiner and Modood, 2002). Within the UK the processes by which this happens are little understood. Thus this book aims to fill the gap by providing insights into how some young black people shape their lives to strive to transform their unsuccessful school career and achieve successful outcomes beyond compulsory schooling (Rhamie and Hallam, 2002; Rhamie, 2007).

The intention of the book is to examine young black people's trajectories; their drive for self improvement, training and employment and the determination to recover from a negative school career. The book will draw on notions of social structure, agency, materiality and resources, structural identities, culture and institutional relationships for example, education, family and community. In essence, the text will provide a distinctive and novel in-depth look at how young black people removed from school respond to challenge and transform their school 'failure' and succeed. Further, the book will reposition the main debates and discussions on risk and fragmented youth transitions to a discussion of the ways that exclusion impacts on young black people's lives. The book will also demonstrate that, although young people are engaged in practices of self-invention and self-regulation, these practices are suffused with notions of the individualising process. This process is reliant on the availability of resources which can have the effect of limiting ambition and achievement (Skeggs, 1997). In the main the book will show how agency, individual response, resistance and challenge are linked to the requisite resources and opportunities made available through social capital facilitated through institutional relationships such as the family, kin and community-based organisations.

Overall, although the book is based on the experiences of young black people excluded from school, it is not strictly about how academic performance is affected by schooling per se. It is instead a study of successes in the black community and uses the issue of school exclusion as a research context. Also, it could be argued that this focus on young black people's success has wider political, social and academic importance. For instance, it raises pertinent questions concerning the link between education, 'race', ethnicity, social justice and social mobility or social stratification in relation to youth in society today. In the political sense the book challenges accepted stereotypes with the display of pro-social behaviour which belies their relative school experience and relative structural disadvantage. These appear to be at odds with the notion of 'problem'. Additionally, it challenges the notion of 'troublesome' youth which traditionally underlies much of contemporary youth policy in both the US and the UK (Cieslik, 2001; MacDonald et al, 2005; Ginwright, 2007) and is predicated on the notion of social justice (Griffiths, 1998, p. 3).

The Structure of the Book

We wrote this book with a potentially wide readership in mind. It is our intention that the ideas and understandings offered within it will be relevant for a range of researchers, academics, practitioners, educational professionals, community workers, students and policy makers. In addition to proposing theoretical concepts and providing a nuanced understanding of how young black people respond, resist and work to transform their negative school experience, it espouses a political and applied aim of contributing to and helping to further develop socially just practices within education. The following outline of the book's structure sets out the content of the remaining chapters.

Chapter 1: Theorising Youth Transitions: The Intersectionality of 'Race',
Ethnicity, Gender and Social Class

This chapter provides the theoretical context to the book. It details
the theoretical framework that informs the data and analysis. It argues
that despite an increased interest within the sociology of youth in
the diversity of the experience of youth, it is necessary to highlight the
relative invisibility of young black people's experience in the literature.
Also, it argues for an integrated approach with the inflections of
the social axes of 'race'/ethnicity, gender and social class. In understanding youth transitions focusing on the British black diaspora
key work is reviewed in relation to the theoretical approach adopted,
notably that of black feminist theorists from the US and the UK,
postcolonial theorists and critical race theory focusing specifically
on community capital, social capital and transformation (for example
Yosso, 2005).

Chapter 2: Resistance, Resilience and Empowering Habitus:
Connecting Identities, Ambitions and 'Success'

Research studies within the field of sociology and the sociology of
education have provided valuable insights into the ways in which
young people construct racialised identities (Brah and Minhas, 1986;
Alexander, 1996; Alexander, 2000) especially within the context of
education and schooling (Mirza, 1992; Fordham, 1996; Sewell, 1997;
Wright et al, 2000; Frost et al, 2002; Youdell, 2003; Dewan, 2005).
However, relatively scant consideration has been given to young black
people's own construction of themselves following their negative
schooling experience and how they transform this into a desire to have
a positive educational outcome.

In focusing on a set of related case studies, this chapter provides a
nuanced understanding of how young black people respond to, resist
and work to transform their situation. Thomson et al (2002) explain
young people's diverse reactions to the significant turning points of
growing up. This is encapsulated by what they term 'critical moments'.
In this chapter the young people emphasise that they learn from
the complex critical moment of being excluded. Their narratives are

suffused with notions of culture, individual agency, subjectivity and becoming. For instance, these narratives reveal the cultivation of a positive racial and cultural identity and determination to succeed among the young black people. This will reflect Yosso's (2005) notion of 'aspirational capital'. Aspirational capital is defined as the ability to maintain hopes and dreams for the future, even in the face of real and perceived barriers (p. 77). In essence, this form of capital promotes resilience and a 'culture of possibility' (p. 78) as a way of responding to personal struggles.

Chapter 3: The Role of Family and Kinship in Achieving 'Success'

Bourdieu and Passeron's (1977) work concerning (re)production of privileges and inequality in education within western societies has provided valuable insights into the role of the family in this process. For example, it is argued that education reflects the values of those who gain most from it, that is the white middle-class families. Within both the US and the UK the black family is stereotyped as lacking the values which are likely to achieve educational success (Fordham, 1996; Reynolds, 2006). On the other hand, the critical race theory perspective, particularly the work of Yosso (2005) and Carter (2005) posits that instead of reading the culture of young black people and their family's engagement as oppositional toward schooling or lacking the dominant cultural capital necessary for academic success, theoretical space should be made for a different set of values and behaviour to coexist. In this chapter we concentrate on the role played by family and kinship in enabling the young black people to transform their educational experiences and improve their life chances. Alongside this particular attention is given to mothers' engagement with the process. Indeed, Reay (2000) observes that mothers' emotional support of their children's academic success transfers to educational and social prestige. The young people in our study argued that their emotional well-being and the ability to stay focused on educational and career aspirations benefited from vigilant maternal intervention.

Chapter 4: Peers and Friendship Networks in 'Success' Making

Although a growing body of literature within sociology and the sociology of education emphasises the role of friendship networks and peer relations in the construction of both racialised identities and educational outcome, little research has examined the role of friendship networks in transforming negative educational experiences and any subsequent social mobility.

This chapter explores aspects of the interplay of the young people's successful transitions and the peer or friendship network. The view that the peer group constitutes a bid for power by marginalised groups lies at the centre of many studies of youth subculture. It has become something of a truism that this striving for control reinforces such marginality and re-creates the conditions for its existence (e.g. Willis, 1977; Sewell, 1997). The black peer group is thus seen more as a cathartic expression of frustrated power and social maladjustment than positive action and control. The chapter shows how friendship networks reinforce their self-worth, reputations and sense of togetherness. Peer groups encourage participants to cope with the stress of exclusion and transform their circumstances.

Chapter 5: Collective Resistance: Community Networks and Social Capital in 'Success' Making

Yosso (2005) critiques the traditional application of Bourdieu and Passerson's (1977) theory of cultural capital as it is used to explain the lower social and academic outcomes of people of colour. According to cultural capital theory their lesser social and academic attainment would imply a lack of cultural capital among members of black communities and would also explain any subsequent social mobility. Yosso seeks to theoretically reposition or centre the experiences of black people in the discourse of what constitutes capital. In doing so the writer 'calls into question white middle class communities as the standard by which all others are judged' (p. 82) and thereby shifts the discourse from its conventional notion. Deficit models are used to explain underachievement and the lack of social mobility among the black communities. Similarly, Akom (2003) and Sampson et al (1999) posit the notions of 'community social capital' and 'critical social capital' respectively as the means by which black communities respond to issues affecting the community. Critical social capital departs from traditional notions of social capital by placing a greater focus on the collective dimensions of community change. It also centres on how developing a positive racial and cultural identity and political consciousness provide an important community and social resource for facilitating activities for change.

In applying the repositioned notions of cultural capital the chapter examines the impact of community, cultural and social capital on young people's transitions. In particular, it shows how community-based organisations in black communities provide the young people with critical social capital in the form of connections to community-based organisations. The organisations' work with the young people included fostering a proactive approach to accessing educational opportunities, strategies for grappling with joblessness, activities aimed at developing a positive racial and cultural identity and a focus on achieving success through personal transformation.

Chapter 6: Youth, 'Race'/Ethnicity and Social Mobility in Contemporary Society

The chapter will use the empirical data to provide some critical reflections concerning the (re)production of educational privileges, inequalities and the implications for social mobility (Cregan, 2002). The chapter will link these issues to the possible barriers created by school exclusion for both successful transitions and social mobility. Further the involvement of non-mainstream institutions, for example community-based institutions in counteracting barriers from mainstream institutions to social mobility, offers a fascinating angle on debates concerning ways in which collective social action (Freire, 1972) can transform structural inequalities.

Chapter 7: Understanding Black Youth: 'Success' and Transitions in Society Today

This chapter draws extensively on themes and issues raised throughout the book that are of theoretical and policy relevance in UK society today. It discusses material from the previous chapters which raises wider issues concerning the extent to which young people's transitions reflect continuing outcomes of structural inequality rather than personal agency or choice. Alongside this there will be discussions of social justice within the context of social inequalities.

1

THEORISING YOUTH TRANSITIONS

The Intersectionality of 'Race', Ethnicity, Gender and Social Class

This chapter provides the theoretical backdrop and context to the book. It argues that despite the established body of work in sociology illustrating the diversity of the youth experience, there are gaps in the literature about young black people's experiences. This highlights the extent to which these young people go unrecognised in youth transition discourses. The chapter addresses a central issue for sociology youth research, namely the importance of the intersection of 'race', ethnicity, gender and social class. These related issues need to be collectively theorised if we are to understand young people's identities and transitions. The chapter begins by outlining the theoretical issues and debates relating to youth which we utilise in the exploration of young black people's transitions. We illustrate how this theorisation within the context of black feminist theorists, postcolonial theorists and critical race theorists focuses specifically on social networks, community capital, social capital and transformation (see for example Yosso, 2005) in understanding youth transitions. It focuses on the British black diaspora.

The chapter begins by outlining the theoretical issues and debates in youth sociology, particularly in the area of transitions, on which we draw in exploring how young black people's experience of schooling shapes their youth transitions. We then devote specific attention to the theorisation of how identities are performed, constructed and negotiated on the margins or in adverse circumstances, focusing on the key thinking in the area we shall be drawing on. Finally, we consider the role of social networks of community, family and friends in engendering resilience, transformation in identities and experiences of social inclusion.

Understanding Youth Transitions Within the Context of Difference and Diversity

It is recognised that within youth research the concept of transition is often used when explaining young people's choices when they leave compulsory education. Indeed, MacDonald et al (2005) point out: 'The value of the concept of transition has been hotly contested in youth sociology' (p. 874) because it is considered questionable whether the term 'transition' is useful in understanding identity in the young (see for example Miles, 2000; Cieslick and Pollack, 2002). As Miles points out there is also the question as to 'transition to what' (2000, p. 10). Traditionally transition refers to the simple movement from education to employment (Cohen, 1997; Ball et al, 2000; Colley and Hodkinson, 2001; MacDonald et al, 2001; Mac-Donald and Marsh, 2005). In this sense, the main concern for youth sociologists is still the economic transition from school to work, reinforcing this as the key to success, adult citizenship and independence (Furlong and Cartmel, 1997; MacDonald, 1997; Ball et al, 2000). It is argued that young people do not see their lives in such linearity (Ball et al, 2000; Cohen and Ainley, 2000; Evans et al, 2001; Jeffrey and McDowell, 2004). Furthermore, the age of transition is an issue (Dean, 1997). Is economic independence reached between 18 and 21 years of age? (MacDonald, 1997; Rudd and Evans, 1998; Ball et al, 2000; Green et al, 2000; Williams, 2002; MacDonald and Marsh, 2005).

Transitions clearly involve unique and varying circumstances and do not just include the labour market but domestic and housing careers and locality (Furlong and Cartmel, 1997; Miles, 1998; Ball et al, 2000; MacDonald et al, 2001; MacDonald and Marsh, 2005). However, it is argued, societally the key to success is still seen as paid work leading to adult independence and the way to achieve social inclusion (Furlong and Cartmel, 1997; MacDonald, 1997; Department for Education and Employment, 1999; Ball et al, 2000; MacDonald and Marsh, 2005; Wright et al, 2005). Indeed, the UK Labour government since 1997 has made social inclusion a stated focus of its policies (Social Exclusion Unit, 1999a) with socially excluded and problematic young people at the nexus of this discourse. Ostensibly, the assumptions underlying this discourse imply that young people are socially excluded because of their attitudes, beliefs and lack of employability. However, the notion of social exclusion/ inclusion at the transitional phase is somewhat problematic. The debates around the use of social exclusion are well documented and it has been criticised for its use as a 'catch-all' phrase to identify people (Halpern, 1999; Ball et al, 2000; MacDonald and Marsh, 2001; Macrae et al, 2003; Stephen and Squires, 2003). MacDonald and Marsh argue that social exclusion is a 'short hand label' to describe particular places and people who live in them (2001, p. 374). Further, the term social exclusion 'carries a set assumptions about the charac- teristics of the people involved and the circumstances of their lives which may well not be true of the young people categorised in this way' (Attwood et al, 2004, p. 77). Moreover, social exclusion is an applied concept rather than one used in self-definition and it is not adopted by young people (Ball et al, 2000). Defining young people as socially excluded not only places an 'othered' identity on them which may impact on a person's sense of self-worth, but also necessitates reference to the included (Sibley, 1995). Furthermore, this construc- tion of young people is reflected in many of the policies and public projects which seek to address those labelled as 'socially excluded' or 'marginalised'. For a critique of the policy agenda regarding this group of young people see Levitas (1998), Ball et al (2000), Hills et al (2002) and MacDonald et al (2005). Interestingly, young people's views are 'often absent from discussions around policy and practice' (Archer and Yamashita, 2003, p. 55) and it is suggested that there is a need to look at the nature and extent of disengagement and the reasons young people offer for it (Attwood et al, 2004). In this vein, it has been suggested that the concept of social exclusion is in need of overhauling in order to reflect more subjective evaluations of those presumed to be experiencing it (Stephen and Squires, 2003).

Young people's transitions have become more complex and less class-bound. Also, as the adult labour market has been restructured, the youth labour market has declined. Further and higher education have also expanded. Within this context, the 'extended transition' into further education or vocational training, from which Ball et al (2000) claim the Learner Society is born, is at the forefront of policies for 16–18-year-olds. The focus on the Learner Society impacts on opportunities for some young people (MacDonald and Marsh, 2001). Various metaphors have been used to describe the 'youth phase'. These include 'niches', 'pathways', 'trajectories', 'navigations' and 'critical moments'. However, MacDonald et al (2001, 2005) argue that 'since the 1970s, youth transitions have become more complicated, extended and apparently less class bound. This does not, however, invalidate the *concept* of transition' (p. 874).

Curiously, it would appear that within a field where there remains a strong tradition of class-based, and to some extent gendered-based inquiry (Furlong and Cartmel, 1997; Du Bois-Reymond, 1998), questions of 'race' and ethnicity tend to be neglected (Maguire et al, 2000). The exception is the work of Claire Alexander (1996). In this regard, it is intended that the book provides a critical contrast to the often colour-blind approaches which characterise youth transitions studies in particular, and British academic youth research, in general (Cieslik, 2001).

Notions of 'risk' (Beck, 1992) and 'individualisation' (Giddens, 1991) lie at the heart of much of the recent work in youth transitions. The notion of individualisation suggests there is an increasing reliance on individual resources and risk. These are considered to be features of late modernity. The notion has been employed by a range of youth researchers to make sense of the increasingly fragmented pathways in the transition to adulthood (Furlong and Cartmel, 1997; Du Bois-Reymond, 1998; Ball et al, 2000). However, it has been argued that changing economic and cultural circumstances 'should not be an excuse for exaggerating "individualized" self making, [therefore] ignoring how structures operate and produce effects' (McLeod and Yates, 2006, p. 224). Indeed, it is acknowledged that those young people vulnerable to class-, gender- and 'race'-based discrimination are most at risk. The concept of 'structured individualism' (Furlong and Cartmel, 1997) dismisses the duality of structure and agency and sees them as interlinked (Mitchell et al, 2001) unlike some policy discourses. Evans' (2002) concept of 'bounded agency' is useful in being able to capture some of the more intricate aspects in the structure and agency debate. This concept highlights that young people can exercise agency in their lives but this is often bound by structured determinants. Yet, interestingly, individualisation is dominant in youth policy discourse. For example, initiatives to engage young people aged 16 to 19 outside mainstream education, training or employment who are identified as 'vulnerable at this transitional phase' (Department for Education and Employment, 1999) have tended to focus on individual deficiencies (Archer and Yamashita, 2003). Unlike the structure versus agency debate which underlies the theorising within youth transitions research in the UK, the intention in this book is to bring a more nuanced understanding of the combined issues of young black people's educational success post compulsory schooling and young black people within the transition process. Thus, this book aims to locate notions of culture and individual agency within an appreciation of intermeshed structural identities and inequalities of 'race', ethnicity, gender, social class and age.

'Race', Gender and Class in Youth Transitions

The individual transition pathways of young people are thus a consequence of personal agency, structure, critical moments, youth culture, economic policies and locality. This section explores how social class, gender, 'race' and ethnicity are also key factors influencing the nature of youth transitions. The notion of 'intersectionality' is pertinent to this discussion. Intersectionality is a term coined by Kimberly Crenshaw (1991). Brah and Phoenix (2004) argue that intersectionality offers a framework whereby 'race', ethnicity, social class, socioeconomic and other social divisions can be theorised as lived realities.

As mentioned above, youth researchers have discussed individualisation in relation to the Risk Society thesis (Giddens, 1991; Beck, 1992) but many conclude that social class, socio-economic status, gender and 'race' or ethnicity are still determinants in young people's lives (Furlong and Cartmel, 1997; Green et al, 2000; Mitchell et al, 2001; MacDonald and Marsh, 2005). These factors can help in understanding the social exclusion and marginalisation of some young people. The situation is more complex than that presented in the theorisations of Giddens (1991) and Beck (1992) which have been criticised for placing too much emphasis on individual reflexivity (Furlong and Cartmel, 1997) and overestimating the role of agency in constructing people's identities (May and Cooper, 1995). It is argued that the abstract individualisations they present do not consider the 'practicalities and expectations faced by people and the "fixities" of labour market structures and demands for qualifications' (Ball et al, 2000, p. 39). Further, Furlong and Cartmel (1997) introduce the idea of an 'epistemological fallacy' to debates of individualisation whereby individual choices and responsibility are reinforced but structural determinants are not recognised. Thus, failure in this context becomes individualised experience. Yet people cannot be detached from the structural constraints which still have influence on life chances and form the 'surrounding opportunity structure' in which decisions are made (MacDonald and Marsh, 2001, p. 383).

Opportunities for social mobility for young people from disadvantaged backgrounds are fewer than they were 20 years ago (see Nunn et al, 2007).[1] Some argue that there are now increased inequalities for some groups in society (Cregan, 2002; Thomas et al, 2003). In particular young people and young people of low economic status are not addressed in government policies. For instance, Thomson et al (2002) point out that the expansion of further and higher education has benefited more the 'not so bright middle class rather than academically able working class youth' (p. 346). Those working-class individuals who succeed rely more on external support than those from a middle-class background who depend more on individual resources, for example, determination or effort (MacDonald and Marsh, 2005). It has been argued that young people have increasingly embraced a 'can do' philosophy: a process of individualisation which is a feature of the UK in the last 25 years. However, a 'can do' attitude may make a difference for middle-class young people but it is not sufficient for working-class young people who lack the social and cultural capital of the middle class (Thomson et al, 2002). Working-class young people are also more likely to have a loyalty to locality which may constrain transition pathways (MacDonald and Marsh, 2005). Parental interventions can lead middle-class young people out of the locality by setting their children on a pathway to university.[2] Middle-class families are also in a position to provide support for a longer period than working-class families, thus perhaps delaying entry to the labour market by several years. Polarisation has become greater in transition patterns between the middle and affluent working class whose transitions last several years and those where transitions are more rapid and potentially problematic (Ball et al, 2000; Jones, 2002; MacDonald and Marsh, 2005). Destinations are then very much influenced by family position along with that of the wider kin group (Furlong and Cartmel, 1997; MacDonald et al, 2005; MacDonald and Marsh, 2005).

The process of transition is not simply a matter of the expression of class cultural values. Goldthorpe (1996) advocates a modified rationalisation theory to help explain why working-class young people leave education earlier than middle-class youth. For example, they make different calculations regarding the costs and benefits of educational possibilities post 16 and have to earn money as soon as possible (Ahier and Moore, 1999). Furthermore, locality very much influences life chances. Local crime, local drug problems and physical deprivation shape local opportunities (MacDonald et al, 2001).

The implications from what has been noted thus far are that choices at age 16 are more critical than in the past. The opportunity of further or higher education usually results in a more certain future. Those who decide to 'take any job now' have a less certain future (Ball et al, 2000; Colley and Hodkinson, 2001; Wright et al, 2005). The gap is increasingly between those with good qualifications and those without (Ball et al, 2000; MacDonald and Marsh, 2005; Wright et al, 2005). However, educational success is not directly matched by labour market success as the experience of many young black people shows (Cregan, 2002). Likewise, educational achievements are not necessarily reflected in women's occupational status or income (Jones, 2002).

For many working-class young people the goal at age 16 is still a job and a partner. However, as a result of changes in the youth labour market noted earlier, there are increasing difficulties in obtaining a job post 16. Consequently some young women are drawn back into the family routine and having a partner and pregnancy as an escape. Young men, unable to support a family may maintain a lifestyle based on alcohol, drugs and crime. These developments also partly stem from the relatively low value many young people place on education but they result in a more pronounced social exclusion in the UK than most of the rest of Europe (Bynner, 2001).

The relatively low value placed on education results in the view that the transition to adulthood, for working-class young people, is primarily about entry to work. As noted above, the lack of employment and the reluctance to continue with education or enter training can result in more females making the transition to adulthood through teenage motherhood and for young males through casual or unskilled work, delinquency and crime. However, changes in the labour market have resulted in an overall rise in job prospects for women. Females are now more likely to be engaged in the job market than in the past as a result of the growth of service sector jobs. The educational achievements of girls have improved more rapidly than boys and far more now enter higher education with a corresponding postponement of marriage and family (McLeod and Yates, 2006). However, for those females without qualifications there is frequently a rapid exit from the labour market to have children (MacDonald and Marsh, 2005). There is thus not only an increasing polarisation between males and females but also between females and males with and without qualifications (Bynner, 2001).

Although studies have identified the role of social class or socio-economic status and gender in youth transitions, relatively little is known about the role of 'race' and ethnicity. It has long been known that as regards the employment of young people of African-Caribbean heritage, they are as a group disadvantaged in four labour market indicators: employment and unemployment rates; earnings; occupational attainment and progression in the work place and levels of self employment. However, there is little information on whether black females and males are following the same types of transition paths noted above.

One way of understanding the differential experience of transition for young black people is to examine the role of education. All young people travel through a transitional period at the point of leaving compulsory education. Increasing numbers of young people now move on to further education, others move into full-time employment.

At the end of compulsory schooling at age 16, approximately 71% of young people stay on in education. By age 18 this is approximately

37%. Twelve per cent of school leavers gain employment and less than 5% gain a government sponsored training place. A further 7% are not in education or employment and the destination of 5% is unknown (Green et al, 2001). Seventeen per cent of school leavers are engaged in employment or government sponsored training but in 1989 this figure was 39%. This change is mostly accounted for by young people continuing in full-time education, realising that entry to the labour market is increasingly dependent on higher skills and qualifications. However, with an increase in participation in full-time education there has been an increase in part-time work among students, reducing the opportunities for those who do not continue in education. At any one time about 10% of 16–18-year-olds are not in education, employment or training (Green et al, 2001). With 60% of 18-year-olds not in education it is clearly the case that young people in the UK spend less time in education than in all other western countries with the exception of the USA. Youth transitions therefore, tend to be more rapid than in the rest of Europe (Bynner, 2001).

A higher percentage of young black people stay on in full-time education than white young people. Sixty-nine per cent of white young people continue in full-time education whereas the figure for young black people is 82%. One reason for this is that further education, that is colleges, offer opportunities and courses for young black people who have been alienated by their experience of school. Young black people are able to be supported by a community of black students. A second reason for this is that young black people are less likely than others to participate in job-related training: 3% of young black people compared with 10% of white young people (Department for Education and Skills, 2003).

However, participation in degree study is lower than other groups. Twenty-two per cent of black adults (16–64-year-olds) are studying for a degree compared with 26% of white adults, 39% of Indians and 30% of Pakistanis. Those of African-Caribbean origin are also more likely to enter higher education with GNVQ and BTEC qualifications than white people or with Access qualifications.[3] A smaller proportion of black people enter degree study through A level than other groups: 40% of black people compared with 68% of white people, 65% of Indian, 53% of Pakistanis. The vast majority of black people in higher education (69%) are female and black people tend to be older than other groups who enter higher education (Department for Education and Skills, 2003). It can be seen therefore that the transition from school to further or higher education tends to be different for young black people than for other groups.

Transitions, Marginality, Resistance and Identity

This discussion of youth transition thus far has implied that transitions are infused with notions of identity. Although social class, socio-economic status, gender and 'race' and ethnicity do define life chances, it is the impact of 'failure' that can be individualised resulting in experiences being constructed in terms of personal deficit. This in turn can impact on the sense of identity and what young people believe can be achieved. This can have a further marginalising effect. It may be for this reason that the focus of many government programmes has been to build upon social skills, personal development and the enhancement of self-identity and self-esteem of young people (Department for Education and Employment, 1999).

Contemporary social theory has a considerable amount to say about people's complex and shifting social identities. For Stuart Hall (1996) identities are multiple, 'never completed, never finished' (p. 5). Identity is always in the process of formation. Giddens' discussion of identity is explored in *Modernity and self identity* (1991). He develops his understanding of self-identity in terms of the reflexive self, the reflexive self here referring to the self understood by the individual in terms of their biography. Black feminists have argued 'identity is not one thing for any individual, rather each individual is both located in, and opts for a number of differing and at times, conflictual, identities, depending on the social, political, economic and ideological aspects of their situation' (Bhavnani and Phoenix, 1994, p. 9). In this vein, while identity can be viewed as internal, personally led and psychology-driven, it is recognised that it has to be located within broader societal constructions and limitations, for example around social categories of 'youth', 'race'/ethnicity, gender, social class/socio-economic status and so on, as well as within social groupings, whether nations, communities or families. Thus, identity is formulated and experienced at the intersection of these internal and external factors. Narratives of identity have increasingly moved towards assertion of open, shifting and multi-forms of identification: of identity defined by choice, lifestyle and performance. Yet, it can be argued, in terms of the representations of young people in public youth policy discourse in the US and UK, political rhetoric and policy practice identity remain much more simple, neatly bound and static.

Within youth research young people's identities are discussed as complex, fluid and fractured components (Ball et al, 2000; Green et al, 2001) of multi-dimensional lives. Many researchers have noted the difficulty in accounting for young people's identities and how research can only provide a limited account of complex and fragmented identities (Ball et al, 2000) and complex, often chaotic biographies (Dean, 2003) in situated social contexts (Raffo, 2003). In this area, there has been a wide range of research exploring young people and their identities: identity within youth transitions (MacDonald, 1997; Ball et al, 2000; MacDonald and Marsh, 2005), identity and youth consumption (Miles, 1998) and identity and risk (Mitchell et al, 2001). However, we need to be mindful that much of the research in this area has been primarily with reference to young white people and white communities and hence care must be taken when extending these notions to young black people.

As previously mentioned in the Introduction, black people in their lived experience of the black diaspora are subjected to unfair and unjust handling by large statutory bodies, of which education is one. As a consequence, identity construction often takes place between assimilation and exclusion (Bhui, 2002). Black feminist work provides a valuable vantage point from which to understand the complex multi-dimensional world which young black people inhabit on the margins of white institutions and frameworks and young black people's agency and subjectivity in relation to their space on the margin (also see Fordham, 1996). Utilising notions of identity, blackness, subjectivity, inclusivity, resistance and marginality, bell hooks points out how the margins can be a radical location in which black people can situate themselves in relation to the dominant group. They have 'other ways of knowing'. Further, hooks argues that we should reclaim the word 'margin' from its traditional use as a marker of exclusion and see it as an act of positive appropriation for black people.

> Marginality is a central location for the production of counter hege-monic discourse – it is found in the words, habits and the ways one lives . . . . It is a site one clings to even when moving to the centre . . . it nourishes our capacity to resist . . . . It is an inclusive space where we recover ourselves, where we move in solidarity to erase the category coloniser/colonised. (hooks, 1991, pp. 149–150)

Similarly, Fraser argues, black people appear to occupy parallel dis-cursive spheres. This sphere, Fraser refers to as 'hidden-counter public spheres which are arenas where members of subordinated social groups invent and circulate counter discourses, which in turn permit them to formulate oppositional interpretations of their identities, interests and needs' (Fraser, 1994, p. 84). This book will explore the ways in which young black people use their past and current experi-ences, namely their damaged 'learner identities' (Ball et al, 2000) and stigma emanating from their negative experiences of schooling to produce positive future identities. In this sense, it is important to recognise the extent to which young people can contest identities that are imposed on them and whether this limits their capacity to repro-duce their own identities. Also, it is important to recognise the extent to which they can negotiate their own eventually successful learner identity, in order to avoid, in echoes of Coard (1971), being marginal-ised, labelled and experiencing feelings of failure.

Transforming Experiences: Transitions, Social Networks and Social, Cultural and Community Capital

Within youth research one way of exploring transitions to adulthood is through the concept of social capital (Bourdieu, 1986). Social cap-ital refers to forms of social participation and connection, such as memberships of networks, groups, communities, families and friends and so on, which provide an important type of resource. This concept is further significant as it recognises that choice and agency are accompanied by the availability of resources, which can enhance or limit achievement and ambition (Skeggs, 1997). Cultural capital, according to Skeggs 'exists in three forms: in an embodied state, i.e. in the form of long-lasting dispositions of the mind and the body; in the form of cultural goods; and in the institutionalized state, resulting in such things as educational qualifications' (2004, p. 16). Previous research has found that families and friends often provide emotional capital for young people (Thomas et al, 2003). It also recognises that structural inequalities circumscribe the range of options open to some young people as there is unequal access to social capital (Archer and Yamashita, 2003; Ball, 2003). Those without social capital are subject to the greatest insecurities (Stephen and Squires, 2003). In this regard, Ball (2003) suggests that the white middle classes are 'adept at taking up and making the most of opportunities of advantage that policies present to them' (Ball, 2003, p. 261). For example, middle-class families are able to 'make the best' of educational choices and access the most elite educational spaces, for example 'elite' schools and universities thanks to their differential possession of embodied forms of social capital. In contrast, the working class lack institutionally valued forms of capital or have the wrong sort of capital. This suggests that for white working-class young people

> paradoxically . . . while local networks helped in coping with the problems of growing up in poor neighbourhoods and generated a sense of inclusion, the sort of social capital embedded in them served simultaneously to close down opportunities and to limit the possibilities of escaping the conditions of social exclusion. (MacDonald et al, 2005, p. 873)

Within black diasporic communities both in the US and UK the development and sustainment of social networks is recognised as vital to reduce the effects of marginality and as a site for genuine inclusion. Moreover, some theorists, particularly critical race theorists, have questioned whether the concept of social capital can best account for the nature and the ways in which black diasporic networks are delivered and experienced. In brief, critical race theory, coined by Derrick Bell in the US, refers to 'a set of interrelated observations about the significance of racism in western society' (p. 32, cited in Gillborn, 2008). It is not the intention here to address fully this theoretical debate. For a full account of critical race theory see for example

Bell (1995), Crenshaw et al (1995), Ladson-Billings and Tate (1995), West (1995) and Yosso (2005).[4] Critical race theory perspective has broadened the scope of the concept of social capital which is used interchangeably with cultural capital. Yosso's (2005) critique provides a common application of Bourdieu's (1986) theory of social and cultural capital: explaining the lower social and academic outcomes of people of colour. According to social and cultural theory their lesser academic attainment would imply a lack of social and cultural capital among people of colour and would explain any subsequent lack of social mobility.

As Yosso suggests,

> cultural capital has been used to assert that some communities are culturally wealthy while others are culturally poor. This interpretation of Bourdieu espouses white, middle class standards and therefore all other forms and expressions of culture are judged in comparison to this norm. (Yosso, 2005, p. 76)

This has led Yosso to ask 'Whose culture has capital?' Instead of narrowly defining (social) cultural capital to include only white, middle-class values, Yosso theorises the validity of community cultural wealth 'an array of knowledge, skills, abilities and contacts possessed and utilized by Communities of Colour to survive and resist macro and micro-forms of oppression' (p. 77).

Yosso (2005) posits six kinds of capital found in Communities of Colour. These are theorised as dynamic and interrelated. First, aspirational capital is defined as 'the ability to maintain hopes and dreams for the future, even in the face of real and perceived barriers' (p. 77). This form of capital promotes resilience and a 'culture of possibility' (p. 78) that pursues increased social mobility. Second, linguistic capital honours the various languages and communication skills that Students of Colour may bring to school, including storytelling, poetry, music and visual arts. Third, familial capital is the 'cultural knowledge nurtured among familial (kin) that carry a sense of community that are not biological kin, resulting in extended communal or "family bonds"' (p. 79). Fourth, social capital includes social networks just as in the definition given above but these specifically include the emotional reassurance needed to navigate new social contexts, for example when helping a family member, biological or extended, to apply to college. Extending from social capital and related to aspirational capital is the fifth form of capital, navigational, which deals with the competencies needed to navigate social institutions which can be racially hostile, for example academia. Finally, resistant capital is defined as 'those knowledges and skills fostered through oppositional behavior that challenges inequality' (p. 80). This form of capital encapsulates many of previous forms because it 'includes cultural knowledge of the structures of racism and motivation to transform such oppressive structures' (p. 80). It draws on the aspirational, familiar social and navigational forms of capital to promote social mobility.

Although Yosso's (2005) theorising of 'community wealth/capital' is within a black American context, it would appear to 'have some resonance in the historical tradition of the [British] Black Education Movement' (Cork, 2005, p. 14). Moreover, several writers (for example Gilroy, 1987; Hylton, 1996) theorise the collective resistance by black parents and children as a form of resistance to structural inequalities experienced across and within institutions. As Gilroy (cited in Mac an Ghaill, 1988) points out:

> Localised struggle over education, racial violence . . . continually reveal how Blacks have made use of notions of the community to organise themselves. Involvement in local community policies provided an insight into theorising the different forms of resistance to racism and authoritarianism within schools, as linked to parents' survival strategies. They made clear their understanding of their children's critical response to school, as part of their resistance to racism. (p. 163)

A significant feature of this collective resistance is exemplified by the black educators, mainly women, who work in black community schools, often referred to as supplementary or Saturday schools (see Mirza, 1997; Cork, 2005). These workers operate within, between, under and alongside the mainstream educational structures, renaming and reclaiming opportunities for black children through the transformative pedagogy of 'raising/lifting the "race"'. In this respect these networks seek social transformation through educational change. Ultimately, the struggle for educational inclusion is borne out by the desire to transform opportunities for themselves and their children.

Moreover, these networks exemplify the black communities' collective desire for self-knowledge and a belief in the power of schooling/ education to militate against racial barriers (Fordham, 1996, p. 63). Indeed, as Freire argues, education is the terrain on which they, the oppressed, acquire consciousness of their position and struggle (Freire, 1972). The literature further suggests that for young black people the alternative spheres of community networks, the voluntary sector and family relationships encourage a positive identity and sense of community in the face of enduring structures of 'race' and class inequalities (Alleyne, 2002). As Perri 6 points out 'networks are not just something individuals can make and use for themselves. They are relationships with many others' (Perri 6, 1997, p. 1). In this vein, this book is concerned with exploring how locally embedded community and social networks become part of the process whereby young black people transform their adverse schooling thereby playing a role in the shaping of inclusionary transitions.

Summary

This chapter has examined the roles of 'race', ethnicity, gender and social class or socio-economic status in young people's transitions. It has looked at how these are theorised in relation to understanding young people identities. The chapter began by scrutinising the concept of transition and its relationship to structure, agency and individualisation. The chapter continued with a discussion of the role of social class and socio-economic status in youth transitions from school to higher education in UK.

This was followed by a discussion of the relationship between transition and identity formation and the understanding of subjectivity and agency particularly for young black people. The chapter ends by using Bourdieu's concept of social capital, particularly how it is used by critical race theorists. There is an emphasis on the importance of networks in transforming the negative experience of schooling to a positive one for young people.

2

RESISTANCE, RESILIENCE AND EMPOWERING HABITUS

Connecting Identities, Ambitions and 'Success'

Introduction

The introductory chapter described how black students are more likely to be excluded from school (Osler et al, 2002; Department for Education and Skills, 2003) and those excluded from school are more at risk from exclusion in wider society (Melrose et al, 1999, in Harris and Eden, 2000; Wright et al, 2000). Yet there has been very little consideration of how young black people, who are excluded from mainstream education, interpret their situation and construct an identity for themselves. This chapter examines how, following negative schooling experiences, young black people who are excluded from school and pushed to the margins, go on to secure for themselves a positive educational outcome. In looking at a set of case studies, this chapter provides a nuanced understanding of how young black people respond, resist and work to transform their situation, in order to emerge with a successful outcome. In doing so, two concepts are considered. The first is Thomson et al's (2002) 'critical moments' and how young people react to these significant turning points in the process of growing up. The second is Yosso's (2005) notion of 'aspirational capital', which is defined as 'the ability to maintain hopes and dreams for the future, even in the face of real and perceived barriers' (p. 77). It is argued that these combine and lead to a form of capital, which itself promotes resilience and a 'culture of possibility' (p. 78) as a way of responding to personal struggles.

Situating Critical Moments

In discussing the relationship between social structure and self, Giddens (1991) highlights the notion of 'fateful moments'. That is 'times when events come together in such a way that an individual stands at a crossroads in their existence or where a person learns of information with fateful consequences' (Giddens, 1991, p. 113). At such times, the individual concerned makes a risk assessment, part of which involves undertaking identity work and drawing on a number of expert resources. In working through these 'fateful moments', Giddens argues that there is the potential for empowerment. Thomson et al (2002) develop this work with their notion of 'critical moments': events described in narrative which are viewed as 'having important consequences' for the young people involved (p. 339). They argue that such 'critical moments' are distinct from Giddens' (1991) 'fateful moments', in that they are events that are reflected upon and in doing so are viewed as having had significant consequences for the life story narrator. In our study, the young people reflected upon their experiences in interviews, some time after they had been excluded from school. Although some of the young people were still in the process of pursuing transitions and harnessing individual agency, most were at a stage when they were able to reflect on a transitional period in the past tense. Having done so, they had stated for themselves that the exclusion from school was viewed as a significant event in their life that had serious consequences, both short and long term. In this sense, the exclusion can be viewed as their 'critical moment' (Thomson et al, 2002).

A number of complex factors combined to create for the young people, circumstances which placed them at increased risk of being excluded from school. As well as being racialised, their experiences at school were viewed as a gendered or class-biased process, or as having occurred within the context of changing family situations. For example, black boys are between four and fifteen times more likely than white boys to be excluded from school (Sewell, 1997; Department for Education and Employment, 2000b) and black girls four times more likely to be excluded than white girls (Parsons and Castle, 1999; Osler et al, 2002). Also, it has been found that the majority of excluded children come from difficult home backgrounds (Bourne et al, 1994; Cohen and Hughes, 1994 quoted in Harris and Eden, 2000; Hayden, 1996; Kinder et al, 1996 quoted in Parsons, 1999; Parsons et al, 1996; Smith, 1998; Harris and Eden, 2000). Although it did not seem as if the young people's family background played a significant role in their behaviour at school, the perceptions of the young people, on the basis of their family background, were that they had been stigmatised by the teachers and schools. This stigmatisation had increased their chances of being viewed as problematic and hence being excluded. For example, one young man who had been in care reported:

> If I had one fight with someone else they would blame me and saw me as the violent one . . . I don't know . . . the teachers just looked at me like this 'oh he's in a children's home and he's got no family so he's out of control'. (Ray)

Although the UK Labour Government since 1997 have considered the complexities and difficulties of young people's transitions in policy making (for example Social Exclusion Unit, 1999a), its education policies have largely sought to address class-based and gender-based issues. Thus, matters of 'race' and ethnicity have largely been neglected (Ball et al, 2000). This is a serious omission because as our study illustrates, for the young black people, there was an awareness of the exclusion being primarily viewed as a raced process. Their perception that it was seen as a 'black problem' was understandable given the widespread belief that black youth are troublesome, aggressive and anti-education (Wright, 1987). This view shifts the blame from a discriminatory education system to argue that black people, especially those of African-Caribbean background, suffer from a deficient culture. This Cultural Deficit Theory is the idea that young black males are also handicapped by a culture which downplays the role of the father figure (Lawrence, in Ratcliffe, 2004, p. 75), and which leads some black individuals, regardless of age, to act in aggressive and challenging ways, for example by responding with a hegemonic masculine identity that exhibits hardness (Phoenix, 2001). Indeed, some argue that black boys in particular draw on youth/street 'gangsta' culture, which incorporates an anti-school ideology (Sewell, 1997), which, although it gives them the collective strength to resist racism, also undervalues academic achievement. Academic aspirations are disparaged as a form of 'acting white' and the living out of this black masculinity inevitably leads to failing to meet the norms of school behaviour. Of concern though is the ways in which the construction of black masculinity in schools then goes on to play an important part in the wider processes of societal marginalisation. However, another explanation emphasises teacher racism (Gillborn, 1998), this being a staffroom culture of racism based on disciplinary problems with previous pupils that lead to low expectations and the interpretation of certain behaviour negatively, which in turn leads to a form of pre-emptive disciplining (Gillborn, 1998).

The young people's sense of unfairness at the exclusion is often exacerbated when compared to the punishment allocated to their white counterparts for the same or even worse behaviour (OFSTED, 2001). This means that in addition to the deviant labels attached to the young person, the exclusion also represents a process of racialisation for young black people, a racialisation process that again represents the practices that they will very likely experience in wider society. This is the construction by the schools and teachers of black students as troublesome individuals, which is associated with the idea that black students are construed as threatening, menacing and the product of inadequate parenting. Indeed, the interviewees had discussed this racialisation process and its unfair consequences:

> They play the white kids against the black ones, being a white child or something, the black child gets in trouble for it and the white child gets away with it, you see them do it and the black child gets in trouble for it. (Earl)

Such educational stereotypical expectations of black young people as troublemakers, challenging and aggressive, have been widely documented (Mirza, 1992; Wright et al, 1998). Here young people have found that the white teachers' and white pupils' low expectations and understanding of black cultures, and their stereotypes of black students as aggressive, athletic and over-sized, plays a significant role in the trapping of black students:

> I felt that because of my size yes and because of my colour, because when they see a black person in their face they feel intimidated. (Ray)

Altogether, 15 of the young people expressed views that racism or racial stereotyping had played a role in their exclusion from school. It should be noted that these views were just as likely to come from those who were of mixed heritage as they were from those of African-Caribbean heritage. Both groups felt they were treated as 'black' and in negative ways.

The exclusion of the young people from school also placed them within a temporary situation of relative powerlessness. This sense of powerlessness was further enhanced by the traditional authoritative nature of the educational system, and later some other institutions that the young people came into contact with, i.e. criminal justice agencies such as the police. Many of the young people already had an awareness of social exclusion, based on discrimination and disadvantage, as some had previous knowledge, whether it be based on fact or myth or actual experiences, either direct or indirect. In spite of this, the episode of exclusion gave the young people and their families direct personal experience of the particularly cruel and discriminatory nature of a powerful system which viewed them as deficient, problematic and, in the particular context of schooling, unworthy of education. Of interest is the ways in which they felt that the official reason given by the school for the exclusion differed from their own perception of the reason. Their perception highlighted instead some of the serious concerns regarding the treatment of young people, in particular young black people, in society today. The young people questioned the school's *real* motive for the exclusion, and raised issues around their accountability, surveillance and punishment of those who do not fit the image of the 'ideal young person' (Becker, 1952).

The most common reason which the young people reported they had been given was their 'challenging behaviour'. The young people had themselves recognised their exclusion as reflecting their non-conformity to the traditional structured process of education and schooling, in terms of teacher authority, the school's quest for accountability and reputation building:

I'm trying to make you understand the climate of the school. The exclusions were coming in fast and furious for anything . . . because OFSTED people were there. (Sirita)

While the school might see the young person as a challenge to authority and to the structured process of education and therefore that the exclusion is fair, for the young people, exclusion is embodied within a process that unjustly labels them as 'folk devils' who create 'moral panics' by threatening social cohesion (Cohen, 1980), that is the social cohesion of the school and wider society. This had been felt by the interviewees who had discussed being inaccurately labelled. For example, in discussing the worst part of being excluded, Lucinda said:

> When they put on my file 'violent behaviour', it just didn't fit. (Lucinda)

Even for those young people who admit a wrongdoing on their part, there is still a sense of unfairness of being labelled inaccurately and unfairly:

> I weren't the only person . . . I admit yeah, I might have been talking . . . but it's not like if the room was silent and I was talking. Everybody was talking and I just got picked out. That's the way it seemed to me. I was the one what got caught yeah. (Antoine)

Transforming Marginal Status

For many working-class young people, the goal at age 16 years is to have a job and a partner (Bynner, 2001). However, despite the rather simple and non-demanding nature of these goals, their realistic attainability had become difficult.[1] This could be due to the high levels of 'unpredictability, back-ward steps and false starts' that young people are now faced with (MacDonald et al, 2005, p. 874). This is especially so for those who are also black, and especially so for those who have experienced exclusion at an early age, for example having been excluded from school. This is because not only are negative labels of black people in general, i.e. as aggressive, lazy, problematic and challenging, being used as a way of viewing the young black people and hence their life chances, but in addition their exclusion from school is being used as a means of 'proving' and reinforcing this stigmatisation.

The effects on the young people of being excluded, in terms of the impact the exclusion had on their self-esteem and sense of self, suggest that a deviant label plays a large role in the young person's perception of self. Young people in these circumstances are certainly aware of the negative stereotyping on them (Archer and Yamashita, 2003), and the difficulties associated with resisting these stereotypes. For example, in cases where school reinstatement had been achieved, the young people explained that they were ostracised when they attempted to reintegrate in schools. They suffered from being ignored by both teachers and other students, who perceived them as trouble-makers and liars, and so not worthy of a place in the teaching and learning environment:

> After [the exclusion] I felt I was labelled and picked on by teachers, especially the head master for little incidents . . . when I got back yeah he would just stop me for anything. (Lee)

The impact of this also had more serious consequences, in that for many of the young people, exclusion from school was a traumatic experience which they felt was a personal attack. This resulted in a loss of dignity and respect. For example Yolan had recalled:

> I went through a phase where [I was] really depressed and I didn't want to go back . . . I just felt bad and I felt like I was unwanted sort of thing . . . like I was just a reject of the school. (Yolan)

These feelings were consistent across gender boundaries, as well as those cases involving young people of mixed race background. However, for those raised in care, being excluded from school had been a particularly distressing event. For example, Ray had talked in depth about his feelings of growing up in a care home and his perception of how he thought others at the school had viewed him as a result of this background, in addition to the racial labels they had placed upon him. This had clearly had a negative effect on how he initially thought about his own sense of self:

> It's the way people look at me . . . they [teachers] would blame my home . . . and when they see me they are like scared of me when I am talking to them, and it's like 'I can't talk to him, he's a black youth, I'm better moving away' kind of thing . . . . (Ray)

In such exclusionary contexts 'people participate in their own empowerment that emerges from self-defining processes' (Graham,

2004, p. 45). The young people in our study made a number of attempts to transform their marginal status via the development of a strong positive self-definition that overcomes the exclusion reputation, as well as counteracting the processes of racialised discrimination and exclusion that they are likely to face in wider society. This meant for some the loss in self-worth is a temporary reaction and in the vast majority of cases it was followed by the development of a resilient sense of self:

> I think what I've been through has brought me to how I am now. I mean if I didn't go through what, what I've been through makes me who I am and I wouldn't be the way I am if I didn't go through what I went through. I think it taught me a lesson. I think I learnt quite a few lessons about myself . . . I was really, really bad, but my experiences helped me to change, made me who I am now. (Matthew)

Many young people reported the awareness and development of a positive racial identity, in this case a positive black identity as an important strategy for surviving the devastating effects of the school exclusion. Resilient black identities motivate young people to renegotiate assigned labels, disprove official expectations of them and instead seek to create their own dignified aspirations. In doing so, the excluded young people renegotiated their temporary battered self-esteem, dealt with the exclusion and tried to reintegrate themselves back into the education system. Graham (2004) argues that this engagement in positive racialised self-defining is particularly important 'in order to decolonise the mind and avoid intellectual enslavement' (p. 45).

It is significant though to highlight that negotiating for themselves a racial identity and in particular, a positive black racial identity, is not a fixed and linear process. It is instead a social process that is based on the renegotiation of meanings, language and symbols (Mead, 1995). It is also, as Jenkins argues, 'never a final or settled matter' (1996, p. 4) but an identity that individuals reflexively work through. Although the allocation of a black label can be applied to individuals in a negative and discriminatory way, the 'internal-external dialect between self-image and public image' (Jenkins, 1996, p. 22) means that individuals are able to reject inappropriate, ill-fitting and offensive labels and substitute in their place more positive and suitable labels. This is what many of the young people in our study reported and, although it was at times a very difficult process, once a suitable racial identity was fostered which in this case, for this moment and, for these young people, was a black racial identity, the pathways for empowering oneself and making successful transitions could be pursued.

The young people also used their consciousness to become empowered black youngsters demanding the rights to an unbiased education. In doing so they challenged racism and emerged with a proud identification with black cultures. Sewell (1997) explains that black youth's sub-cultural responses to threatening images of black young people are now either being internalised or redeveloped. This black consciousness enables young people to have the positive self-awareness and pride to reject racist stereotypes at school. They do so by reconstructing self-perceptions that confront white teachers' authority. Although there are perceived differences in how males and females are treated by the excluding school, similarities have been observed in the ways in which both genders respond to the teacher's treatment of them, in that both males and females were prepared to confront and challenge teachers (Callender and Wright, 2001).

In particular, black young women effectively reassert black self-determination and academic achievement, by demonstrating a commitment to schooling and a resistance to racism without risking conflict (Fuller, 1984) or teacher confrontation (Mac an Ghaill, 1988; Callender and Wright, 2001). Consequently, the black female's dedication to equality, independence and responsibility not only allows her to control her self-definitions, but also to assert positive self-definitions in the place of negative ones. Although covered in more depth in the next chapter, it is useful to note here the long history of black women having created for themselves a 'culture of resistance' (Collins, 1990) and in particular for their male family and community members a 'home place' as a 'site of resistance' where, in the face of discrimination and disadvantage, a 'safe place' could be created 'where black people could affirm one another and by doing so heal many of the wounds inflicted by racist domination' (hooks, 1991, p. 42). Such sites also act as cultural resources and sites of political activity. For example, consider the response by the mothers and sisters of the men who were convicted of rioting and disproportionately punished (in comparison to the white rioters) in the civil disturbances that occurred in 2001 in the northern UK cities of Oldham, Burnley and Bradford.

In the case of their male counterparts, although feeling equally demotivated by the exclusion, they are more likely to initially respond by displaying the perceived black hegemonic masculinity which leads to even more negative attention from teachers (see Sewell, 1997; Callender and Wright, 2001; Phoenix, 2001). After this initial response, the males then assert positive self-definitions, via for example, an attempt to 'prove teachers wrong':

> My mum and dad just said, when I was excluded they just said . . . the main thing . . . was to turn the negative into a positive in the long run by what I did, what I achieved, my exam results, which was basically like spitting in the head teacher's face. (Roger)

This also has a forward looking characteristic, in that the young people become more focused on their studies and career prospects. For example, Leon had said:

> I want a decent job . . . and anything that pays . . . then look for an office job when I get a bit older like and wear suit and tie and everything . . . it's not like I'm dumb . . . I got plans. I got ideas for the future. (Leon)

In outlining the 'Risk Society Thesis', Beck (1992) and Giddens (1991) emphasise that those who are black and located at the lower end of the class spectrum, are far more at risk than others from uncertain and complex youth transitions. Of these 'risk' groups, those who are additionally excluded from school are much more at risk from detrimental long-term social exclusion (Wright et al, 2000). An accumulation of the denial of suitable education, the stigmatisation as problematic and untrustworthy and the reduced social contact with school peers, resulting from the school exclusion combine to contribute to the wider social alienation of many young people who have been excluded from school (Melrose et al, 1999, in Harris and Eden, 2000, p. 6). In having challenged the school exclusion label through the renegotiation of negative racial labels, young people are aware that their experiences of school exclusion are more than likely to be mirrored in wider society. For example, as one young person commented:

> If you want to go somewhere you have to dress normal if you've got hoods and trainers on people think you are out to cause trouble. Sometimes when I go into town and I've got jeans on and an ordinary coat they don't follow me [security guards in the shop]. As soon as I go in with my hoods and trainers they come heavy. It's like that every time . . . I don't want to wear normal clothes. I want to wear what I like, why should I change my appearance for other people . . . I have to be happy in my clothes. (Keenan)

It is argued that young people who are excluded from school are more likely to offend than those not excluded (Graham and Bowling, 1995) because 'with a vicious circle of bad behaviour and rejection, through the process of labelling and self-fulfilling prophecy . . . a destructive label of "excludee" or "disaffected child" can cause delinquency to emerge in a new form – criminal activity' (parent of excluded youngster, in Harris and Eden, 2000, p. 66). Indeed, just under half of the young people interviewed for the study reported here had been involved in offending behaviour: 15 of them reported having received either a conviction or a caution. However, the majority of young people who commit offences tend to grow out of their offending behaviour (Graham and Bowling, 1995). For many young people though, doing so can be difficult and troublesome. This is because not only do the young people have to deal with the consequences of the exclusion label (i.e. troublesome) and the pathological stereotyping of black people but they also have to make the transition in a disadvantaged social environment where they are located at the lower end of the class spectrum, lacking in the availability of economic funds and investment and recorded as a high-crime area. This means that overcoming the risk of (further) participating in offending behaviour is the outcome of them having bounced back and forth between (i) the internalisation of the deviant label, (ii) the rejection of the deviant label, (iii) the renegotiation of the deviant label, (vi) a lapse in the control of the deviant label via the participation in offending behaviour, (v) the (re)management of the deviant label, (vi) the (partial) removal of the deviant label. For example, in discussing his experience of getting caught up in committing offending behaviour when excluded whilst trying to manage the exclusion label, Will had said:

> It's hard because being out of school leads to committing crime because you're out of school and ain't got nothing to do . . . and what I'm saying is that the kind of person I am I am easily misled by friends . . . because I'm free . . . I don't live at home with my mum, I live in a children's home. (Will)

However, even when some young people's development of a positive self-awareness reduces their offending behaviour, they nevertheless acknowledge that they will continue to face exclusion with such 'others' who play a large role in the allocation of deviant labels, such as the criminal justice agencies and the police:

> They [police] said I was supposed to have robbed someone . . . because I have been arrested for it before they are saying that it's my description . . . but I know loads of people who can pass for the same description. (Christopher)

The current population of young people's continuation of full-time education has been largely attributed to their realisation that entry to the labour market is increasingly dependent upon higher skills and qualifications. This in effect means that transitions into adulthood are difficult, in that the excluded young people follow more fragmented, extended (Cohen and Ainley, 2000) and non-traditional pathways. Most of these pathways see the young people being stuck in a 'magic roundabout' where they go through various training schemes, casual employments, petty enterprise, quasi criminal activities, 'cash in hand' fiddly jobs, periods of unemployment (Green et al, 2001) as well as other stages of 'ambiguous dependency' (Ahier and Moore, 1999). The young people had recognised that the exclusion equalled a damaging affect on their education and thus hindered their employability chances. For example, when talking about the effects of the exclusion:

> It's a downfall for a job. (Will)

This is primarily because the lack of educational qualifications is seen as a barrier in the competitive nature of today's labour market. As a result, the excluded young people feel that they are limited in their ability to apply for certain jobs:

Obviously when you go for a job they always ask you what your school is and what qualification you have. If you ain't got none, or can't remember like your last school, that's bad. (Antoine)

However, excluded young people have been shown to continue to exhibit high levels of optimism in terms of finding work and achieving career aspirations, which in turn helps them to gain control over their transition into employment (Rudd and Evans, 1998). For example Earl who had discussed his NVQ in Music Technology and his plans to do a two-year music course at college, had said:

I am going to put my head down and get a career in music, and get a proper job.

These levels of optimism have the potential not only to produce positive outcomes for the young person involved, but also for their immediate community. For example, Nembhard and Pang (2003) in their US study of black youth who had experienced educational marginalisation, found that despite often coming from 'families with low net worth and communities that lack economic opportunity' (p. 187), their sample of students were proactive in the creation of self-empowerment organisations which assisted their pursuit of educational inclusion and addressed wider issues of exclusion, discrimination and social justice. They were also engaged in community building which enhanced the social and economic capital of the community.

In our own study, the optimism demonstrated by the young people for making successful transitions into employment was more likely to be realised by those whose families had the economic status through which the young person could access particular resources. For example, David, who had described himself as 'middle class', had recalled how his parents had been able to buy him a PC (Personal Computer) so that he could develop his music skills:

Well my mum and step-dad bought me a PC so I can like make music at home and that. So they are actually spending money into helping me progress then. (David)

However, whatever their economic status, most of the young people attempted to counteract any limitation in choice by using the available resources around them and their own self-determination in order to enhance their options. They did this primarily by going back into mainstream education, going into further or higher education, or taking part in specialist training courses. All these pathways were embarked upon by the young people with the long-term view that their completion would increase the young person's employability and career development:

> I've done my work experience and I'm doing Business and Finance now
> ... I want to go to university and study a degree in Business and
> Finance. Then hopefully get a job like in Financial Services or an
> accountant or something in that area. (Lucinda)

Although the young people in the study recognised the importance of continuing education and using specialist agencies like job centres and workshops offering advice on making applications for their job-search strategies, other research carried out by MacDonald et al (2005) found on the contrary that their sample of young people considered informal methods of job-searching to produce the most effective results. Such informal methods included utilising personal networks consisting of family members, friends and neighbours to gain advice or to provide recommendations for local vacancies. Although it should be noted that the present study also found that the types of employment being gained were in, as MacDonald et al state: 'the lower reaches of the service industries and routinised, factory production . . . They were the jobs that individuals laboured at when they were 17 and when they were 27' (p. 881). Although the young people in our study recognised the importance of the need to find employment, especially in an increasingly competitive market, they were also driven by the desire to secure for themselves a career related to their interests and one which would allow promotion.

As well as hard resources, such young people are seen to benefit from having been embedded into their immediate close-knit social network. MacDonald et al (2005) argues that these networks are viewed as being important for young people, especially young women. In this network, family members, friends and school peers all come together to provide a source of support. This is despite some instances of strained and tense relationships (Cohen and Hughes, 1994, in Parsons, 1999):

> They [family] kept me up and encouraged me a lot, and yeah, they were always there for me and from the beginning they all believed in me and what I told them. (Tamara)

Similarly, relationships with the young person's immediate black community had largely been positive, with the young people finding them understanding, helpful and supportive:

> I'm getting help from my teachers and school, my mum, grandparents, brother and sisters, friends and so on. They are all very supportive. They'll go onto the internet and find stuff like colleges, application forms or work placements and so they are supportive in that aspect. (Sirita)

Collins (1990) asserts that such mutual respect as demonstrated by the excluded young person's families, friends and communities, is pivotal to black people's empowerment. They are also instrumental to the young person's reclaiming of respect and self-love. The young people reported that families provide love and emotional support, in addition to a much-needed discipline. Friends reinforce their self-worth, reputations and sense of togetherness. Peer groups encourage them to cope with the stress of exclusion, reinstatement and reintegration into education. Uplifting local communities restore acceptance, security and faith in the young person's abilities. Religious organisations give the spiritual guidance, strength and nurturance that enable the excludees to combat exclusion.

Pursuing Positive Outcomes

Research on post-compulsory schooling in the USA has found that despite some negative experiences, black youth are making successful transitions into higher education (Shiner and Modood, 2002). In the UK, the literature has documented how this is also the case for young people of Asian background (Gillborn and Mirza, 2000; Archer and Francis, 2007; Gillborn, 2008). It is argued that young black people in the UK, like their Asian counterparts, are making successful transitions beyond post-compulsory schooling. They are doing so in the continued face of an oppressive and discriminatory educational system which seeks to pathologise them, their families, community and culture. Unlike Fordham (1996), who in her US study of schooling success found that the young black people were relinquishing elements of their black culture and identity in order to succeed at school, our study found that young black people are making successful transitions through harnessing the resources and capital found within the black community. This source of support is further explored in Chapter 5.

What was clear is that all the young people spoke positively about their pursuit of a positive outcome or the setting of goals that would assist them in overcoming the exclusion label. This reflects Yosso's (2005) notion of 'aspirational capital' (p. 77), in that resilience and a 'culture of possibility' (p. 78) were being demonstrated. Here the young black people demonstrated their resistance and resilience to their negative schooling experiences. They did this by utilising agency and structure found within the black community, to overcome the stigmatised labels of troublesome and unworthy of education. This also involved developing for themselves a black identity and positive sense of self. The young black people's harnessing of such resources and identities to develop pathways to success enables them to succeed, break from destructive patterns and to overcome the challenges of a discriminatory education system (Rhamie, 2007).

This is explained by the concept of 'habitus' (Bourdieu, 1986). This is the view that on being excluded, the individual agents, in this case, young black youth, develop a system of certain dispositions: perception, thought and behaviour, in response to the objective conditions of the social field in which they find themselves, in other words the exclusion from school and in wider society. Such individuals share a group habitus because they are the products of the same objective conditions. In this case, the school exclusion is one shared experience. Other shared experiences derive from their wider experiences of racial discrimination and disadvantage and a history of a black diaspora. This common habitus means that the young black people experience very similar dispositions. In addition though, they often develop in these situations very similar responses when combating this disadvantaged position. As hooks notes: 'it is an inclusive space were we recover ourselves' (1991, p. 150). Thus, of significance here is Fordham's (1996) argument, following her US study of education and achievement, that black educational success is not only based on desire and ability, but even more on the process of resistance nourished and facilitated in these safe spaces. Such resistance, as we have found in our own study is particularly embedded in the different child-rearing and gender socialisation practices found within the black family, community and culture (Fordham, 1996).

It is important to recognise though that such processes of resistance and de-stigmatisation are difficult. This is because initially, the exclusion is widely viewed by the excludees as having detrimental effects on how they view themselves and how they perceive others view them. Here, Goffman's (1963) consideration of 'stigma' is of relevance. The term *stigma* is used to refer to an attribute that is seen as deeply discrediting. Those who experience stigma also often feel some related emotions, such as shame, disgust, guilt, depression, rage, humiliation and embarrassment (Nussbaum, 2004). In sociological analysis, stigma is seen as social process involving a language of relationships, not attributes (Goffman, 1963, p. 13). Those individuals who do not depart negatively from the particular expectations/events are referred to as 'normals' (Goffman, 1963, p. 14). Goffman's 'normals'

> believe the person with a stigma is not quite human. On this assumption [they] exercise varieties of discrimination, through which then effectively, if often unthinkingly, reduce his(her) life chances. We construct a stigma theory, an ideology to explain his(her) inferiority and account for the danger (s)he represents, sometimes (using this perceived danger in) rationalizing an animosity [towards them]. (p. 15)

Furthermore, Goffman argues, 'we may perceive his(her) defensive response to his situation as a direct expression of his(her) defect, and then see both defect and response as just retribution for something (s)he or his(her) tribe did, and hence justification of the way we treat him(her)' (p. 16). Clearly, we can see how the major function of these stigmatising strategies is to establish the 'them' and 'us' principle. It is concerned with establishing those deemed within a value structure which is considered good and in favour, and those considered bad and out of favour (Foucault, 1973 quoted in MacDonald et al, 2001, p. 4).

Being excluded from school not only brings stigma, but it also represents a key stage in the young person's transition into adulthood, because it signifies the point when that transition could become a transition into social and psychological insecurity (Parsons and Castle, 1999). It is a transition that could not only damage the young black person, but could also be regarded as another element in the social pathology of the black family (Sivanandan, 1994, in Parsons, 1999) and the black community. For Richard in particular, this awareness ran in parallel with the damaged representation of black people, in particular black males in wider society:

> It's like some white people are threatened by young black people, doing like what you are doing. If you're walking down the street a lot of people try to give young black people a bad name . . . a lot of people are afraid of you, young black people . . . not so much females as lads. Like you're walking down the street people cross the road or you walk in the street you'll see people tripping over themselves to get out of the way . . . it's their problem really. (Richard)

For some the exclusion represented a critical moment in their life which had created a change and awareness in their attitudes to issues around exclusion, racism and empowerment:

> I think that because I'm black, I have to try extra harder than my white counterparts especially and because of what happened to me within school as well, people can refer back to that and say 'yes' and use that as a justification for labelling me in the future . . . so I have to work that bit extra to avoid it. (Roger)

They also developed a more responsible and mature attitude in terms of their outlook on their own life. In doing so they gained control of the direction of their transition into adulthood:

> I would say I'm more mature and I would not do some of the things that I have done in the past . . . I do want to succeed . . . I'm more focused now . . . in what I want to achieve. That's how I survived the exclusion. (Richard)

The critical moment of the exclusion also led to changes in the young people's behaviour. Being excluded from school led to a determination by the young people to change their behaviour in order to succeed in the attainment of educational qualifications and hence prove their worth:

> I proved them wrong . . . because they weren't expecting me to get one, and I got nine GCSEs . . . so they were shocked. Even the teachers said to me 'well done, I was shocked' . . . I feel like I've challenged them. (Lucinda)

For some young people, a change in behaviour alongside a change in attitude was seen as a more tangible illustration of their mature and responsible self:

> But like I fixed up from that stuff nowadays, I've grown up. I'm just thinking when I look back at it now, it was just funny really like I was stupid, I was a shit . . . nowadays I just don't really like trouble, you get me? What's the point, don't get you nowhere. (Clifford)

Over a third of the interviewees moved to another school following their exclusion and two-thirds were in further education at the time of being interviewed. Almost half had gained some qualification at the time of being interviewed. Some young people had felt that they had a talent, which they did not want to waste. Hence despite the lack of educational qualifications obtained at age 16 years, many nevertheless sought to return to education, or gain permanent employment. In describing the driving force behind his decision to return to education:

> I've got a brain up there right and I want to use it and I don't want it like wasting away. (Anthony)

Some were aware of the negative stereotypes around black culture, and had wanted to disprove these. In particular they had sought to contest and resist the labels of unworthiness, being problematic and unteachable:

> I just want to prove them wrong and I want to show them that they can stereotype as much as they like but that at the end of the day it's not necessarily true. (Tamara)

This left the young people with the knowledge that they had a stigma label. Goffman describes such stigmatisation as the spoiling of social identity (1963, p. 156), where the individual can respond in one of two ways: passing off as normal or covering the stigma (Page, 2000). Indeed, it has been argued that the impact of stigmatising attitudes on the stigmatised individual can vary in form and intensity, but often involve consequential patterns of discrimination and prejudice, which serve to separate and exclude individuals from society and from many of the benefits of society, such as an equitable access to education (Barn, 2001). It is therefore a form of social exclusion. At an individual level the impact of stigma and social exclusion can be devastating. According to Spicker (1984) stigma damages dignity, creates barriers to access (to social services/resources) and leads to experiences of degradation and rejection.

It is very difficult to replace or remove a label, especially a stigma label. This is because such labels become a part of our lived experiences, a part of one's life and one's identity. Replacing such a label is by no means an easy task. This transition involves working through one's life experience. This 'working through', or in many cases a recognition and a desire to 'work through' the stigma label, was observed in the study reported here. Here, the young people's self-perception acted as a significant factor in the overcoming of stigma and in pursuit of success in transitional pathways. The sense of injustice they felt drove their determination to overcome the exclusion label and to succeed. One way of doing this is by rejecting the stigmatising representations of themselves and developing more affirming representations of their community and culture, and hence develop more positive version of racial self:

> I think that being black and that the reception that you get from other people sometimes it affects you and it can either make you weaker or stronger, and I think in my case it has made me stronger . . . I think in a way it's kind opened my eyes a bit more . . . like I've got to face problems in my life but sometimes it's not going to be an easy way for me to get out of it, I'll have to face it like head-on and deal with it . . . I suppose in a way it's kind of made me stronger like because I'm less afraid to put my opinions across and stronger in the way that I cried about it but now I don't think I would again. (Tamara)

For some, a spiritual dimension was instrumental in increasing their self-awareness, self-respect and resilience:

> and God as well, because at the same time I was going through that patch, I used to read the bible a lot, my mum told me to read certain Psalms, she used to say before I go to school I read certain Psalms and when I come home I read it as well . . . after that incident I made sure that it was done every single day I read the bible . . . it made me feel stronger, like, cos in the bible that I read it's got a certain titles like it would be like if you're worried or angry and then just to do with that certain mood. It makes you feel a lot better, so I'm like I can just do anything. (Lucinda)

In developing self-esteem and a positive identity the young people also highlighted the socially constructed nature of their identity development. Hall (1996, p. 4) argues that although 'identities are never unified and . . . are increasingly fragmented and fractured; never singular but multiply constructed across different, often intersecting and antagonistic, discourses, practices and positions'. Hence, identity, including racial identity, is something that is of a multiple, diverse and context-specific nature, i.e. depending on factors such as physical features, immediate and wider social networks, religion, history and geographical location, for example, and the status of which is ever changing (Patel, 2008). This also means that individuals not only emerge with an identity that is shaped by others in society, as Symbolic Interactionists also argue (Blumer, 1969; Mead, 1995), but also that they navigate towards an identity that they feel is appropriate or of most benefit at that particular time. In the case of the young people we studied, the development of a black identity in particular assisted the resurrection of self-esteem and self-worth. This black identity drew upon the available social capital, in particular the relationships with family and kinship. As Reynolds (2004) emphasises, although this can be used to 're-affirm a Caribbean ethnic identity, they are simultaneously engaged in developing processes, strategic social networks and models of cultural syncretism that allow them to create ethnic identification across ethnic/racial and national boundaries' (p. 13).

It is important to note also that the black identity which the young people did develop is not in accordance with traditional essentialist thinking, that of a core black self that is fixed and determined. As Brah (1996) rightly notes the term 'black' 'can have different political and cultural meanings in different contexts' (p. 98). Hence, usage of such racialised labels, including those that are self-assigned 'is determined not so much by the nature of its referent as by its semiotic function within different discourses. These various meanings signal different political strategies and outcomes. They mobilise different sets of cultural or political identities . . .' (Brah, 1996, p. 102). An additional consideration is how there were also other factors which intersected with the black identity, i.e. gender, class, etc., which impacted on the *type* of racial identity that the young people developed. Here, Crenshaw's notion of 'intersectionality' (1991), also highlighted by Hall (1996), is of relevance. Intersectionality refers to the view, as supported by Gilroy (1987) and Anthias and Yuval-Davis (1992), that racial, ethnic, gender, class and national identities, for example, combine with one another in complex and flexible ways according to the social, historical, political, cultural and symbolic contexts in which they are located. It follows that although black women at the intersection of 'race' and gender have different structural and qualitative experiences to that of white women (Crenshaw, 1991), there also exist intra-group differences. So, for example, it is not correct to assume that two people of the same racial background, indeed even from the same biological family, with the very similar experiences, would actually identify themselves in the same ways as each other (Patel, 2008).

This is supported by Wallman (1979, pp. 5–6):

> two sets of people with common cultural origins placed in similar minority positions [will not] necessarily use the same elements of their traditional culture to mark themselves off from non-member 'others'. What they do use will depend on the resources they have, on what they hope to achieve (whether consciously or not) and on the range of options available to them at the time.

Recognition of intra-group differences also provides an updated consideration to the claims about the double oppression experienced by all black women, or the triple oppression experienced by black women who are also in positions of poverty (Prins, 2006). The consideration of intersectionality in the process of categorisation and identity development also allows for its marginalised subjects to challenge and renegotiate existing labels, in place of more fitting, positive and empowering ones (Prins, 2006). This gives them some choice over the 'politics of naming' (Crenshaw, 1991, p. 1297), because what they are doing is redefining the 'nominal identity' (name) and the 'virtual identity' 'experience', so that they are both embodied by the pursuit for empowerment and equality. This 'naming' of a black label in its politicised sense can also be utilised and mobilised to provide one way of fighting racism. It also allows whiteness and white privilege to be dislodged from its position of desire, power and authority (Patel, 2008).

Summary

This chapter has considered the key issues arising from the young people's perceptions of the impact and their involvement in the school exclusion process. It has argued that individual circumstances and life events, or what Thomson et al (2002) term 'critical moments', are significant in how particular young people follow a specific transition pathway. There are a variety of critical moments that may prove significant. These include changing family situations such as the death of a parent, parents separating or parental unemployment, or relationship changes, such as new friends or breaking up with a partner at a crucial time. The single occurrence of a critical moment can be just as powerful as the accumulation of a variety of critical moments over a particular period; both forms can be highly significant in the choice of a specific transition pathway. Although previous studies have discussed the role of critical moments and how they affect individuals and groups, little research has looked specifically at the experiences of black people. This chapter has addressed this gap. It has done so by discussing young black people's experiences of school exclusion as a critical moment in their transition pathways. Additionally it has highlighted the importance of the school exclusion as a significant critical moment that leads to changes in attitude and behaviour in how the excluded young people see themselves, and the decisions they make in attempting to make a successful transition into adulthood. The exclusion as a critical moment had been experienced in very similar ways and had similar meanings for the young people. Although the young people acknowledged that something they had done had led to their exclusion, they expressed an overwhelming sense of injustice which was exacerbated by the belief that punishment was also racialised. These culminated in a number of effects, including a loss of dignity, respect and self-worth. However, it is important to recognise that these are temporary feelings, as many young people develop a positive black identity as a strategy to disprove official expectation of them. Although they found it a struggle to overcome some of the negative aspects of school exclusion, such as the reduction in the likelihood of being employed, increased police attention and pressures on relationships with family members, friend and peers, the young people were able to reinforce self-worth and transform their marginalised status.

3

THE ROLE OF FAMILY AND KINSHIP IN ACHIEVING 'SUCCESS'

Introduction

Cork (2005) argues that 'Black parents feel marginalised and their concerns are often ignored. There is a need for partnership with schools (who) need to focus on raising standards and look for support from parents, community and Black teachers' (p. 111). This chapter considers the importance of this agenda. It does so by focusing on the roles played by the families in assisting the young people to help regain control over their lives. In presenting some narratives highlighting the value and strengths of such support, an insight is also given into how under such pressures and strains, members are able to come together to transform the disadvantaged position of the excluded young person. This is done by transforming their educational experiences and improving their life chances. The key themes and issues identified include coping with exclusion by adopting an attitude of perseverance and by giving support to the young person in the form of acceptance, advice, and practical help. The effects of the exclusion in terms of wider relationships and the culture of respectability is also examined. In doing so, the chapter considers the work of Reay (2000) who observes that mothers' emotional support of their children's academic success transfers to educational and social prestige, as well as the contribution of critical race theory, for example, the work of Yosso (2005) and Carter (2005) who argue that for the achievement of black and minority ethnic academic success, a theoretical space should be made for a different set of values and behaviour to coexist.

The family can be viewed as a key institution in society in which the needs of its members and wider society are provided for, in that it not only raises offspring, catering for their survival requirements, but also socialises them, instilling values and the skills necessary for them to develop into healthy people who can contribute to a prosperous society (Lambert and Streather, 1980, pp. 19–20). However, here a particular type of family is seen as the productive ideal. This is western society's views of the nuclear family. The traditional classic model of this nuclear family is that it consists of the father who is the head of the household and economic provider; the mother who is the homemaker and provides domestic care and socialises the children, and the helpless and dependent children, whose emotional, financial and welfare needs are met by their parents (Raport et al, 1977, in Lambert and Streather, 1980, p. 19). This family type is held up as the ideal and when variations are presented, they are held as problematic and undesirable. Negative views about the black family partially emerge from their supposed clash with this ideal of the 'normal' family, and when difficulties emerge, they themselves are blamed and punished for the disadvantaged position in which they find themselves.

An opposing view is that the black family is one of the key agents for assisting successful transitions, particularly by acting as a site of support and nourishment for the development of positive and healthy identities. In this sense it is referred to as 'familial capital', which is a variety of kinship, including both immediate and extended family members and even friends (Yosso, 2005, p. 79). Additionally, hooks (1991, p. 43) argues that the construction of a 'homeplace' as a site of 'resistance and liberation struggle' has contributed to the resistance of the black family. This was best illustrated in the UK in the 1950s onwards, by the response of the black community in the Southall area of London, which demonstrated patterns of self-reliance and community support in response to poor local and national state service delivery (Institute of Race Relations, 1981). In the US, during the same time, this was also demonstrated by the Black Power Movement. Here, a growing body of studies have been undertaken highlighting in particular the strengths and resilience of black family units. For example consider the works of Hill (1971), Logan (1996), Smith (1996), Genero (1998) and McAdoo (1998) in the US and

Hylton (1996), Modood et al (1997), Small (1998) and Prevatt Goldstein and Spencer (2000) in Britain. These studies highlight that despite a past history that has been filled with racial oppression in the form of forced migration, slavery and genocide, these oppressed communities have through struggle, resilience and mobilisation of strengths, survived and in many cases thrived. Indeed, hooks (1991, p. 47) even argues that such a 'domestic space has been a crucial site for organizing, for forming political solidarity' against racist aggression.

The family as a site of empowerment and as an instrumental force in the excludees' successful transition was highlighted by the interviewees in this study:

> My mum was helping me, she's there all the time for me, she was pushing me like 'you need to get back into another school or centre or something at least to carry on your education' and she did help me and she came to the interviews and everything, parents' evening, she was always there, so, I had good support from my family . . . She (mother) was the one, if she weren't here then I would have just felt, I don't know, I would have just felt that I can't be bothered anymore, it's not worth it but she was just there telling me 'don't give up, because you'll get somewhere soon, you'll get somewhere in life'. (Miranda)

In addition to providing support, family members also acted as role models for the young people, demonstrating the realistic achievability of positive goals:

> I would say the person that made a lot of impact for me was my sister, going to university and living the lifestyle, going away. I admired that in certain ways . . . I thought if she can do it, I can do this then . . . I can't make her (sister) pass and then I fail . . . because that's going to spoil the pattern . . . so I had to keep the pattern going. (Roger)

The Impact of the Exclusion on the Family

In our study, as in others (Parsons et al, 1996; Pomeroy, 2000) the impact of the exclusion of the young person from school has been found to have serious detrimental effects on their families. All in the reported study stated that the exclusion was a difficult and stressful time. Indeed, this has been highlighted by some of the narratives presented here.

Like the young people, family members had viewed the exclusion as unfair. For example:

> It wasn't justified. At the end of the day it went through a court of law and he was found not guilty. What he was accused of he hadn't actually done ... [but] the [school] governors aren't going to side with the parents, they side with the head teacher. (Father of Richard)

Although these feelings of unfairness had angered family members and had been emotionally difficult for them, it had also been a key factor in their determination to clear the young person's name or help them overcome the exclusion:

> I found it a terrible, terrible, terrible time, I found the whole thing really, really traumatic ... I don't know if it was the initial shock of him being excluded to begin with ... it was very traumatic for me, I was nervous, I felt very nervous at the time ... but I knew on the outward I had to be strong, I had to go about the right channels and look at the different means to help him with the appeal, but on my quiet moments I felt within myself like a wreck. (Mother of Roger)

For many, additional stress was caused in families seeing the difficult time that the young person was experiencing:

> Coming up to five weeks or so when he was off school, I thought 'no, enough is enough' ... I could see Earl getting depressed at home because all his sisters were getting up and going to school ... I started going up to the school and sometimes one of the teachers would bring homework here for him and I'd have to take it back up to the school. It started to stress me out as well. I just didn't have Earl to look after. I had three other children at home as well. It started to get me down, stresses, watching him going through all that stress as well. (Mother of Earl)

Some people though, felt they had coped with this difficult experience:

> They [appeal panel] were very rude, they were unwelcoming as well, but I'm a strong natured person, so I was able to cope with such people, you know, not be easily intimidated at all ... I thought to myself, my daughter, she's a bright child so I was more determined that no, I'm going to prove them wrong. (Mother of Lucinda)

It is not surprising that all the families reported that the exclusion had affected their relationships with the young person. Such a profound experience undoubtedly will lead to a variety of pressures and strains on familial relationships:

> It was like she had PMT 24 hours a day. I'm telling you, you couldn't control her. She was out of control. It got to the point where I left home . . . and left her in the house on her own and let her survive . . . all I done was put electric in, gas, and make sure she had food . . . I even got reported to the council that I left her in the house . . . basically it got to the point where I could not live with her. (Mother of Rose)

In some instances, familial relationships had temporarily broken down:

> They [young person and siblings] were fighting all the time. It got to the point where they were arguing and fighting, because of the problems and situation . . . it was unmanageable. Then she [sibling] left home. The other daughter, the eldest one, she left home as well and moved into a flat on her own. (Mother of Rose)

However for the majority, making attempts to resist and overcome the exclusion actually strengthened the relationship between the young person and the family:

> It made us closer . . . he was able to open up a lot more to me. (Mother of Gavin)

Not only did the exclusion affect the immediate family's relationships with the young person but it also affected the relationships that they had with extended family members and others in the community, from whom many of the young people received support, advice and guidance. Such support was also given to the young person's family. This had strengthened the relationship between the young person and their immediate family member.

In discussing the culture of respectability and class, Skeggs (1997) argues that 'respectability is one of the most ubiquitous signifiers of class' (p. 1). For many black families, however, in addition to the class factor, a culture of respectability largely exists on a racial level, both within the black community and within wider society (Dove, 1998). To develop and maintain such a respectable status, the black family is required to disprove negative ideas about them such as being dysfunctional, disrespectful and pathological. Black families who experience school exclusion report that there is a sense of shame attached to the exclusion label. This shame and stigma then hinder their status and respectability, particularly within their immediate community:

> It is difficult to describe how embarrassed you feel. You get angry with the child as well, it's just nature, it's natural to say 'why, you know better'. (Mother of Richard)

The process to help the young person overcome the school exclusion label is driven not only by a desire to prevent the young person from facing further exclusion in wider society but also to regain and maintain the family's respectability status within the black community.

Left in Educational Limbo

Of prime concern for family members was the fact that once the young person had been excluded they could be left with no educational provision and with no indication of when this period might end. This has also been found in other studies, for example the Prince's Trust (2002). In our own study, while some of the young people and their families had been lucky enough to be able to readily and quickly access the necessary support and resources, allowing them to get on to community projects and pupil referral units, many had been seriously let down by the statutory provision that is supposed to advise and guide the young people and their families through the exclusion process. The consequence of being left in such state of limbo had a significant impact on the young people and their families. Some young people had been left at home with nothing to do. They were suspended in uncertain territory while waiting for a decision about their education:

> They stopped at home for months, not go to school. For weeks they don't go to school. (Grandfather of Ray)

Being excluded at such a key stage in their education, being given inadequate support from statutory provision and being faced with such an indeterminate state had the potential for devastating effects on the young people's education:

> No support [from the school]. They [school] sent some stupid homework which was not really adequate, was not revision. Then he missed out on all his revision. (Mother of Lee)

Although it is the responsibility of the school to send work home to the excluded young person or to make arrangements for the work to be collected, schools often fail to do so (Hayden and Dunne, 2001). This was found to be the case for many of the young people interviewed here:

> I had to be phoning them up to send homework and sometimes they didn't send any . . . I phoned the school all about this, you know, I've been up the school and can't get in touch with the teachers, I can't do this. I've phoned the school 'oh yes, we'll send the papers', nothing is sent. So they reckon he'll fail anyway. (Mother of Lee)

In spite of these experiences many of the young people's families had continued to believe in the value of education. This is because education is seen by black families as an important and valuable necessity (Mirza and Reay, 2000).

For some of the families, teachers were helpful:

> Even when Earl was excluded he (teacher) said to me that if I wanted he would come and give Earl extra tuition, for him to catch up with his work, which I thought was quite nice of him. (Mother of Earl)

Rhamie and Hallam (2002) in their study of black academic success in the UK found that a crucial determinant of success was if school teachers had high expectations of the black youth and offered endless support and encouragement to young people. However, most of their sample of black youth had experienced more problematic relationships with their teachers. For many, their teachers were described as 'uncaring, unsupportive, hindering examination and career aspirations and in some cases being racist' (p. 8). Similar feelings have been reported in studies on young people who come from single-parent (matriarchal) families (Dove, 1998; Blair, 2001) and working-class backgrounds (Blair, 2001).

Interviewees in the present study echoed this view:

> The system has failed him, he's been de-motivated completely. (Mother of Richard)

School Exclusion as Racial Discrimination

Hill (1971) argues that there are five key strengths of the black family, which have been culturally transmitted from one generation to the next: a strong kinship bond; a strong work orientation; a strong achievement orientation; flexible family roles and a strong religious orientation. Others after Hill (for example, Hylton, 1996; Sudarkasa, 1997; Jones et al, 2002) have also supported this view. It is therefore argued that the black family has a unified outlook that is based on years of having experienced and survived racism. This outlook allows them to assess risk, project protection, build up an effective wall of resilience, and harbour success for its members. As hooks (1991) comments in her discussion about the black family 'homeplace': 'With this foundation, we can regain lost perspective, give life new meaning. We can make homeplace that space where we return for renewal and self-recovery, where we can heal our wounds and become whole' (p. 49). This strength is partially due to the unique ability of black families to retain strong familial links with members in both Britain and abroad, and the ability to act as a positive black role model for children (Cheetham, 1986; Rashid, 2000).

The educational system's negative stereotyping of black families as problematic and in particular its pigeon-holing of black youth as underachievers, problematic and unteachable has been well documented (Gillborn and Gipps, 1996; OFSTED, 1996; Mirza and Reay, 2000; Reay, 2000; Blair, 2001; Rhamie and Hallam, 2002; Wright et al, 2005). Here there is a tendency to racially individualise underachieving rather than consider the racially discriminatory behaviour of the education system itself. This was endorsed by interviewees in the present study:

> She had a fight with a white girl, the white girl accused Lucinda of stealing her mobile phone, which evidently she didn't. The white girl, because she's white and she goes to one of the Catholic schools . . . the

teacher you know, they're racist, I have to say it plainly, they treat the black girls differently from how they treat the others . . . they excluded Lucinda and not her . . . to be honest I just said to them 'well, you know I believe my daughter, you believe your staff, I believe my child and the reason why you do this is because she's a black child, not any other reason' and that's me, I just come out frankly with the, you know. (Mother of Lucinda)

In addition, racial discrimination was also considered to be compounded with class:

The teaching and the teachers have a white middle-class view of the black child . . . which is fuelled by the media, and I don't really think some of our kids stand a chance. (Mother of Roger)

This awareness is significant in that it was considered to be a reflection of the type of discrimination that is illustrative of practices in wider society:

They [black people] can't get to the top because there is always people stopping them from getting up there . . . It is still hard for the black youths of today, one because they can't get a job, two the police think because they are walking around in gangs right they are up to something . . . it makes no difference what colour skin we are, we are all equal but we are not treated equally. (Mother of Rose)

In addition to the exclusion labels placed upon the young people, reports have been made of the families perceiving a racist bias when, as is often the case, appearing before an all-white panel (Harris and Eden, 2000). For example, in talking about the way in which she had thought the school and appeal panel had viewed her son:

They [the appeal panel] saw Gavin as a stereotypical black youth, because he's very dark, he doesn't smile a lot, he can look very intimidating because of his colour and I just think they put him into a category before they even saw him . . . I do believe it is a 'race' issue and I think when you're dealing with black youths and families they know nothing about our culture, they know nothing about us at all. (Mother of Gavin)

This perception is particularly so for single-parent mothers who believe that their children are further discriminated against because they are from single-parent (matriarchal) homes (Dove, 1998). The male-headed nuclear conjugal family type, dominant in the western world, is still viewed in Britain as the preferred norm. Hence other family formations are viewed as dysfunctional and problematic (Carby, 1982; Dove, 1998). Indeed many of the interviewed single-parent mothers had felt that when called before such panels, they had themselves been labelled in this way:

> They [school] said of me that I was a dysfunctional, abusive parent.
> (Mother of Sirita)

The families then had to defend themselves as members of the black community and symbols of black culture in situations where they felt they were under attack, when in such panel meetings.

In talking in depth about methods of struggle against such pathological black stereotypes, families had utilised a number of techniques. The first stage of this struggle included recognising such attempts at pathologising them:

> It's hard I'm telling you now. It is hard. It's hard for a black person because you got to work twice as hard as a white person . . . racism has been around for a long time and it's not going to go away. (Mother of Rose)

Further, instances of having to navigate perceived demeaning experiences of panel meetings can be found within this quotation:

> The last meeting when they said you had to go to the unit place is when I had to stand up and tell her [panel chair person] about how she [teacher] was behaving and I didn't like what she was doing to my child and what she was doing to the black children, basically I called her a racist . . . she had to sit there and take it . . . and she was sitting there, in other words the impression she is giving is you're black, I don't care you mean nothing to me, no matter what you say, I'm not going to change. That's the impression she was giving . . . I had to put her . . . [the teacher] put her in her place . . . and I put her in her place. It's another thing when you go to school they always expect the black parents to go on badly . . . I never gave them that satisfaction, not once. (Mother of Yolan)

Replacing the existing pathological labels of them assigned by the schools and wider society (Rhamie and Hallam, 2002), with more accurate and positive labels of 'tenacity', 'integrity', 'dignity' and 'survivability' (Dove, 1998, p. 164), enables families to manage the young person's school exclusion, and the black family's wider social exclusion. Many of the families felt that the value and importance of the black extended family unit needed to be appreciated more as a site of struggle against discrimination and oppression. As such, greater encouragement and support, as opposed to damnation, needs to be given to black families:

> We [black families] need to come together and share ideas and experiences . . . that's how we learn and that's how we can get help and sort out our kids. (Mother of Lucinda)

The families also noted the help and support that the young people and their families had received from voluntary organisations that specialised in working with black people. Here it was said:

> I think that it is good, you know the black groups helping black people, and you find as well that there are some people who don't know about these organisations and what is going on, and also people who have got mixed raced kids as well they don't know where they can go for help. Because they are probably not getting help from schools . . . we need more black teachers, we need more black politicians who are going to help, and more black organisations. (Mother of Rose)

Here the role of mentors has been found to be of particular value (Klein, 1995). However, in our study it was also commented that more positive black role models needed to be found in society, role models that were readily available, visible and fairly represented in all areas:

> Because all the black teachers in this school, like, they don't motivate the black children, to say 'oh this is your history, you can do this or that', whatever, like they have to prove something to the white teacher that they're not on the black children's side and this is the problem. They [children] have nobody to face as a role model who is like them . . . (Mother of Lee)

Social and Cultural Capital

In their study of white working-class areas in the UK, MacDonald et al (2005) found that individuals were experiencing social exclusion through residing in areas where there was high unemployment, problems of crime and drugs and general social decline. However, they argue that there was a '(largely) unquestioned acceptance of the normalcy' of these exclusionary experiences (p. 880). Although there were feelings and some evidence of inclusion in the form of family ties and social network bonds, MacDonald et al (2005) argue that often this led to socially excluded individuals not wanting to leave their neighbourhoods. This suggests that they did not want to overcome their excluded position. Indeed Perri 6 (1997) argues that this is a serious problem and as such, 'we must not celebrate . . . any kind of network or social capital . . . [as some] may be very damaging' (p. 21). However, for the black young people in our study, social and in particular cultural capital, was seen as a valuable resource for overcoming the excluded position.

In a society where 'powerful societal hierarchies within the notion of "know your place", which refers to the ways in which "racialised" structures deny the opportunities and resources' (Graham, 2004, p. 51), the social and cultural capital of the black family is often viewed by mainstream society as being weak and negative for its members, i.e. single-parent households where there are absent fathers, etc. In reality though, the opposite is true. This was found in our own study. Here the availability of social and cultural capital is seen as a key determinant upon the successful transition of an excluded young person. This is because through its notions of rights and responsibilities, community civic engagement and social action (Graham, 2002; Goulbourne and Solomos, 2003) can be collectively mobilised in favour of the interests of its group members. The 'bonding' support that this capital (Reynolds, 2004, p. 5) offers is viewed as helping the young people deal with their problems with school exclusion and their (likely) exclusion in wider society, by providing guidance and stability by listening to, believing, respecting and defending them. What Reynolds (2004, p. 10) refers to as 'trans-atlantic family and kinship relationships', with members in the Caribbean and outside of the UK national boundaries, also assists in the maintenance of a strong and positive identity. It does so by providing a form of social resource to reaffirm membership, connection and belonging to a Caribbean ethnic identity (Reynolds, 2008). All this combines to help the young people realise their self-worth and potential (Thomson et al, 2002). The resources accessed by the young people to overcome their exclusion had transcended gender and class factors. It had also transcended their differences in backgrounds regarding whether they were of single African-Caribbean heritage status or whether they were of mixed race background, as it had their background of familial composition, such as whether they had been raised in care or in a single-parent family.

Practical support had been given by family members in a variety of ways. One way in which practical support was given was in terms of helping the excluded young person with learning, accessing and using resources:

> I came into the school and I sat with him in the library and we studied those extra subjects, so we're talking about the physical education . . . and so I came in, and we did extra work. I went out and bought books, we went to the school library, you know . . . they wanted to expel, they wanted him out of the school, and I said no, so that was a compromise, and my boss allowed me to work particular shifts so that I could go to the school on particular days, whatever lessons, whatever periods they were. So that's what I did . . . I mean, we had a good time because I learnt how funny my son was. (Mother of David)

Hence David's mother had taken on an adapted version of a 'para-professional' teacher role. The most common para-professional role sees the parent acting as a voluntary classroom assistant, who has some degree of power and control, but who largely assists the teacher in the delivery of the curriculum (Cohen et al, 1994). However, the adapted version of the para-professional role that David's mother took saw her focusing her assistance on helping her son overcome the exclusion label, by working on a one-to-one basis. Clearly for David's mother, having the appropriate level of education to assist her son allowed this. Similarly, having the economic capital to access such resources and work as a voluntary para-professional was an important determinant:

We've provided materially for him. We've made sure he's got what he wants to excel in school . . . we wanted to give him a chance. (Mother of David)

David's parents had also been in a financial position to seek legal advice immediately following the exclusion from school:

'Cos he [step-father] cared and wanted to help me out of the situation. (David)

The available economic capital is an important factor to the accessibility of support and resources. Orr (2003) argues that this is because just as limited parental wealth (economic capital) can act as a barrier to the availability of educational resources and opportunities, increased parental wealth can act as a significant key. For example, wealth can shape the young people's academic achievement through influencing their motivation and aspirations (Natriello and McDill, 1986; Orr, 2003). Wealth can also determine the quality of the young people's school, and their ability to move to another quality school after the exclusion (Orr, 2003). Further, the availability of economic capital can give access to study aids and resources such as books, computers, tutors and so on (Jones, 1984; Milne et al, 1986; Orr, 2003). Finally, having the economic capital can allow the young person to be stimulated with cultural capital such as attending arts performances, concerts, exhibitions in order to develop a positive self-image (Orr, 2003).

The lack of funds to assist reintegration into mainstream education and management of social exclusion was a recurring theme in the interviewees' accounts:

I wouldn't be at college because at the end of the day I'm not going to college to find I didn't have any money to get there. I'd rather not go . . . No resources to go to college . . . She [mother] paid my auntie £30 a week to look after me. Out of that £30, I didn't get nothing for college . . . I'd say as soon as you're 16 grab it while you can because you know when you're 16 to 19 you've got every opportunity . . . grab all the courses. That's because at that stage you get a grant. When you are turning up on time you get a grant but when you turn 19 it sorts of stops. (Bernard)

For some the lack of financial resources exacerbated the racial factor:

The bottom line of it and I've realised, it's not so much about being black you know, it's about being poor . . . I went into the schools, what support that they actually give the poor children in the bottom band, on the bottom set, bottom group, to what they give the top, middle to top children, they've prepared them for this, that . . . it's not necessarily about being black, but because you are black and you are poor, it's even worse. They have no hope for you. (Mother of Sirita)

Regardless of the financial resources available, family members could act as advocates:

I've been to a meeting. I asked what they were doing in their school work. (Grandfather of Ray)

It has been argued that parents need to be given better information about the exclusion and its appeal system (Harris and Eden, 2000). Many of those interviewed had sought to cope by becoming better educated about the exclusion process, their rights as parents and their children's rights:

Every human being has rights . . . so I had to find out Tamara's rights in school, my rights as her parent, what I can do for her. So once I knew those, I then know what route to go down. (Mother of Tamara)

Crozier (2001) argues that such involvement by black parents is not recognised in an institutionally racist education system.

Another way parents could help was by having provided positive emotional support by emphasising a parental protective view, either by making comforting assurances that they would resolve the problem, or by providing comforting and soothing emotional support, or emphasising an overt expression of belief in the young person. Parents had also offered the young person practical advice about coping strategies:

I just said whenever he feels that they are winding him up, just to sit down and count to ten, just try and ignore them. (Mother of Earl)

Some had offered advice and used their own experiences as an illustration. Parents' views of the schools are often influenced by their own past negative experiences of schooling (Wright et al, 2000; Blair,

2001). These shared experiences help the family member understand and advise the excludee:

> Like I said to him that there are two roads to take in life. I've done that road, you understand me? I've been down that bad road. (Mother of Keenan)

The emotional support provided by black mothers is particularly noted by black young people as being of key significance in assisting them through to a successful transition (Reay and Mirza, 1997; Reay, 2000). Indeed, the emotional support provided by the interviewed families was driven by a desire to help them overcome the exclusion label. For example, in talking about how extended family members assisted in providing such motivational emotional support, Roger's mother had said:

> The others were very supportive of him. I think that was part of the thing . . . everyone was really, really supportive of him, because when you look at what happened and what it was they [school] labelled him or excluded permanently, we all knew that Roger was not what they say he was you know. We just had to go forward. I said to Roger, 'you have to move forward, you can't let this predicament get you down'. (Mother of Roger)

Focusing on only the immediate family members overlooks the support that was available from wider contacts. As mentioned above there has been a long tradition of community-led initiatives in the shaping of the young black person's successful transition into adulthood (Weekes and Wright, 1998). These 'provide Black youth with critical social capital, which consists of intergenerational ties that cultivate expectations and opportunities' (Ginwright, 2007, p. 403). This was illustrated by Nelson who had talked about the help he had been offered by members of his community:

> I just know they're there . . . it's most of them from round here, they all ask me if I'm ok and help me . . . they say to my mum 'if he want this and that I can help'. It's nice really cos they're on my side. (Nelson)

A small number of the excluded young people had mentioned that they had received support from sympathetic teachers from their excluding school. For example, Tamara had said:

She sent me work to do . . . she's one of the teachers that has always been there for me. (Tamara)

However, despite all good intentions of the teacher, pressures from the excluding school had meant that such support was usually short-lived.

Some of the young people had been raised in care. This had meant that they had been allocated at least one social worker, which many saw a substitute for a parental figure:

The social worker's like your parent basically. (Ray)

These social workers had provided the young person with emotional support and advice:

I don't know, it just upset me when I had to leave [care home] . . . they all liked me. I don't know, I do miss them . . . they supported me really in everything. If I'd be upset she'd talk to me. (Rachael)

In response to an excluded status, black communities have responded by establishing their own initiatives, designed to meet their needs (Reynolds, 2004). Although these modify according to space, time and context, as well as the intra-ethnic diversity of the group's needs (Modood et al, 1997), they are recognised as being of great value for its members and expected to have a 'long lasting influence' (Ahmed, 2005, p. 98). Such 'significant others', which include family and non-kin, not only offer care and support for their members (Manns, 1996), but also impose duties and responsibilities on members (Goulbourne, 1999, p. 176). This facilitates collective action. In our study, the initiatives specifically set up and run by members of the black community, designed to cater for the needs of young people, have also been beneficial to the positive self-identification of excludees and their successful transition into adulthood:

I just woke up one day and thought, what should I do? So I went to [community organisation], I needed to speak to somebody. I feel like I needed to speak to someone. He [agency worker] goes, oh yes, whatever. So I sorted it out, we met three different times. I spoke about everything. He was telling me about my relationship with my mother. Made me feel a lot better. (Bernard)

In addition, the importance of religious faith and religious groups for making positive contributions to coping with exclusion should not be underplayed (Duneier, 1992; Channer, 1995; Rhamie and Hallam, 2002; Alex-Assensoh, 2004). A number of the interviewees spoke of the value of religion in increasing their self-awareness, self-respect and resilience. Similarly, the local church has often been reported as being a vital source of support and comfort by boosting the young person's self-confidence and self-knowledge about their black history (Rhamie and Hallam, 2002). Talking about her daughter's membership of the local church one mother said:

> She's learning about black history there too. (Mother of Sirita)

In illustrating the value of social and cultural capital found within the black community, it is argued that such forms of agency and structure are used by the black young person to develop resistance and resilience to their exclusionary experiences. This is done so successfully that the strength of these 'interpersonal ties' (Granovetter, 1973, p. 1361) should be recognised and used to understand the links with macro-level forms of social mobility.

The type, nature and quality of the support that is made available (and accessed) by the families in helping to overcome the exclusion process, is seen as a key determinant upon the degree to which the outcome is successful (Orr, 2003). Family members had sought support from a variety of statutory and voluntary resources. Statutory resources included mentors that were attached to the school, social services and educational psychologists. For some, these statutory resources had been helpful:

> His social worker was a source of help. I don't know how he's been so lucky because she is still supporting him. I don't know how she does it and gets away with it. She has bent over backwards . . . I owe her so much. (Mother of Anthony)

However, many had found the support from these statutory resources to be inadequate:

> I even went to social services and asked social services for help and I'd been there three times, 'come back the next day and we will sort

something out', so I went back, was there for a couple of hours giving us the run around . . . then they said 'she's your child, you have to look after her yourself'. (Mother of Rose)

Ways of Coping

The young people's families had therefore reacted to being sidelined by mainstream education and by the statutory provision by seeking to empower themselves. They did so by seeking help from voluntary community organisations, through the process of appeals against the exclusion, and by demanding educational rights for the young people:

> I think [Gavin] felt he was on trial, but it was down to his mum and [the Director of CEN] to plead for his innocence because at the end of it we weren't gonna let [Gavin] down. (Mother of Gavin)

As well as being driven by a need to help the young person's self-esteem by resisting the exclusion label, families had also found emotional strength in their desire to overcome negative stereotypes about the black family and the black culture:

> Every day I think, every day I thought I couldn't deal with it . . . but I know I had to, Gavin was the one that kept me going because I could see the rapid deterioration in him . . . he weren't going to be another statistic because he's black and he's young, you know. (Mother of Gavin)

At times perseverance was met with additional hostility and obstruction from the excluding school. The families responded to this however by becoming even more determined to succeed:

> I went up the school one morning . . . he [headmaster] saw me sitting there and I went at eight o'clock in the morning. He was doing nothing, just standing up there. I saw him at twelve o'clock in the afternoon, he came out and he said to the receptionist 'tell Mrs. Smith to make an appointment because I've got lots of things to do', so I turned round to him and said 'it's me who's Mrs. Smith, so you can talk directly to me', he said 'oh, can you just make an appointment', so I said 'no, I'm waiting', I said 'it's my child, so I will wait'. (Mother of Lee)

For many, a belief in the young person's version of events and the blood ties that existed between the families and the young person had been a strong driving force behind their determination to succeed:

> Because he's my child and I knew, with all my kids, they will tell me the truth . . . it [belief] gave me strength because I was saying 'I can't fail my son in this'. (Mother of Lee)

For Anthony's mother in particular, this belief was later confirmed when he was cleared of the teacher's accusation that he had made a sexual comment to her:

> Eventually they found out that she [teacher] lied and he had done three months in prison and got put on the Sex Offenders List for nothing. (Mother of Anthony)

Summary

This chapter has examined the social and cultural capital offered by the young person's family, friends, various support networks, and the wider community, in helping them to transform their excluded position and to make successful transitions. In particular, the impact on the family was examined. Here it is observed that family members were generally optimistic about education before the exclusion, and so were devastated when the young person was left without any schooling provision at all. It was found that exclusion puts a considerable strain on families involved as children are at home all day. There was a negative effect on siblings and a fear of the excludees becoming involved in crime. Despite this strain, relationships between the excluded young person and their family were often strengthened. Families also reported the negative effects on their respectability in the black community. It was found that post exclusion, families still believed in the value of education but had negative views of the education system. This involved the system's negative labelling of black children and young people and their families. There was also a belief in the role of racial discrimination and discrimination against single-parent families. Families therefore sought to challenge the exclusion label. They tended to believe the excludees' version of events leading to exclusion. This was either because they were suspicious of the school's motives, or the role of racial discrimination in the process, or because they did not believe their child was capable of the alleged behaviour. After being excluded, the family reported cases where their child experienced long periods without education. Any alternative provision that had been provided by the LEA was often deemed inadequate by the families, particularly for those children who had embarked upon coursework for external exams (i.e. GCSEs). In response to this, the families devised a variety of methods to cope, in terms of overcoming the exclusion label and assisting their child with successful transition. These included seeking help with appeals, utilising other education options, drawing on support from mentors, social services, voluntary organisations and the church, developing their own knowledge about the exclusion process and the family's rights, and providing the young people with advice and motivational support, or referring to their own experiences. Families' experiences of the exclusion process reveal they have a poor deal from the education system. Black families feel under threat and attack. The sense of belonging in the black community encourages achievement and success for the excludee and helps families overcome the negative effects of exclusion.

4

PEERS AND FRIENDSHIP NETWORKS IN 'SUCCESS' MAKING

Introduction

The previous chapter highlights that withstanding the ongoing impact of school exclusion is dependent upon the resilience the young people developed through parents, home and community experiences.

This chapter explores the young people's eventual transitional success and the role of the peer or friendship network. In this regard, the chapter shows how friendship networks reinforce their self-worth, reputations and sense of togetherness. Peer groups encourage participants to cope with the stress of exclusion and transform their circumstances.

Youth, Peer Groups and Identity

The extent to which peer groups and friendship networks shaped students' ability to perceive, take or decline educational opportunities and aspirations has long been recognised in the fields of education and sociological youth cultural studies where the focus has been on the extraordinary creativity of various groups of youth in responding to their positionality. Indeed, the analysis of creativity in identity construction, identifications and alliances arguably has now become the major focus of sociological studies. For instance, the subcultural model[1] focuses on explaining the connectedness between school-based peer groups, students' response to schooling, the production of masculinities and the persistence of white working-class inequality and, to a less extent, sexual and racial inequality (McRobbie and Garber, 1976;

Willis, 1977; McRobbie, 1990; Mac an Ghaill, 1994; Sewell, 1997; Wright et al, 1998; O'Donnell and Sharpe, 2004). However, less attention has been given to explaining how the peer group shapes youth culture and lifestyles beyond post-compulsory education and into young adulthood.

One of the most influential studies of the potential significance of the peer group in shaping students' adaptation to schooling is Willis' (1977) research on groups of young white working-class males who formed quite distinct groups within the dominant culture of the school. The main group, the 'lads', reject the values of the school and those who conform to it, the 'ear'oles', and further despise those who find academic success, the 'dummies', as well as recognising the potential role of the peer group in drawing students away from formal education. This has been examined in relation to white working-class boys who achieved far less academic and career success than boys of middle-class origin. The performance of boys of upper-class origin did not receive comparable attention.[2]

Studies of young black female and male peer groups chararacterise these groups in a variety of ways. Fuller's (1982) research on young black female comprehensive school students noted that they achieved well academically, despite being members of groups that exhibited 'anti-school attitudes'. Mac an Ghaill (1988) in his study of young black women's response to schooling, describes the mixture of rebellion and acceptance displayed by the 'black sisters' group, which was considered to resonate with the historical survival strategies found among the oppressed. Gillborn (1990) asserted that black female subculture exhibited the strategy of resistance and accommodation which revolved around protecting younger students from experiences of sexual harassment and racism suffered at the hands of teachers. Similarly, Mirza (1997) showed how black girls can inadvertently be pushed together into groups which are perceived as loud, naughty, confident and overtly sexual and how this means that they are inevitably negatively stereotyped along with most other groups who are identified by others as black. Wright et al (2000) suggest that the discourse of black female groups as troublesome and exhibiting openly resistant attitudes to schooling has contributed to their disproportionate involvement in the school's sanction system. This is evidenced by the fact that young black women are four times more likely to be permanently excluded from school than white young women (Osler et al, 2002).

More recent work has explored the production of black masculinities in order to explain the male student response. Sewell (1997) explains how the peer group was found to have played a role in shaping the response to schooling. In order to succeed, aspiring black youth had to assume a form of 'racelessness' and lose their community and ethnic identity to avoid the wrath of their teachers. The young black men who exhibited 'retreatism or rebellion' were not necessarily less positive about learning than girls. However, teachers in Sewell's case study had not only gendered these young men but were obsessed with the changes of black male sexuality. As Frost et al (2002) also found, young men constructed popular masculinities that privileged 'hardness', 'coolness' and an 'anti-school' attitude. The demands of 'hanging out' with friends took precedence over academic work and respondents differentiated between 'bad boys' and 'proper clever' or 'goodie'. Moreover, this masculinity is viewed to be at the basis of the pattern of school exclusion experienced by this group. It is also evidenced by the tendency for young black men to be between four and fifteen times more likely to be excluded than white young men (Wright et al, 2005).

It is argued that, for young black men, often the pressures of masculinity continue beyond post-compulsory education. For instance earlier studies by both Pryce (1967) and Cashmore (1979) remark on the significance of the male peer in black young culture as a response to personal failure and frustration, a retreat to a collective identity. Twenty years on Alexander (1996) focused on an older group of men, between 22 and 24 years of age. This study provided many illustrations of the varied and creative responses to discrimination and frustration experienced by the young black men. Further, the work offers many useful insights of how ethnic culture, including particular images of masculinity, is a major resource drawn on by young black men in the development of their identities and coping with problems and challenges.[3]

That the peer group constitutes a bid for power by marginalised groups seems to lie at the centre of many studies of youth subculture. The black peer group is thus seen more as a cathartic expression of frustrated power and social maladjustment than positive action and control. Below we provide a more nuanced understanding of peers and friends in the lives of the young people. What we found was that peers and friends are significant within all the young people's narratives although their significance can be both positive and negative. As discussed in Chapters 3 and 5, many of the young people in the study mentioned several resources which provided social and cultural capital (Bourdieu, 1986) and aspirational capital (Yosso, 2005). This often included peer or friendship networks.

Peer Groups in the Shaping of Exclusionary and Inclusionary Transitions

In sociological youth literature there is a body of work that emphasises the need to locate young people within their situation-specific context (Ball et al, 2000; MacDonald and Marsh, 2001, 2004). Thomson et al (2002) explain young people's diverse reactions to the significant turning points of growing up and maintain that young people control their life chances with the support of their families and friends. Essential to this source of support is the notion of 'emotional capital' defined by Nowotny (1981) as 'knowledge, contacts and relations as well as the emotional valued skills and assets, which hold within any social network characterised at least partly by effective ties' (p. 148). Although families and friends differ in their access to emotional capital, nonetheless, friends also displayed the ability to mobilise and display emotional involvement and support.

From the young people's discussions of their experience of exclusion and the influence of the peer group, what is perhaps most striking about the young females' and males' renditions of school is their similarity to numerous descriptions of young black people's experiences that have been published over the past three decades (Coard, 1971; Fuller, 1982; Wright, 1987; Mirza, 1992; Sewell, 1997; Gillborn and Mirza, 2000; Majors, 2001; Wright et al, 2005). Here positive reflections on the school were few and brief, whereas criticisms and complaints were numerous and extensive.

The view that the school itself, and the education system more generally, contributed to their exclusion and marginalisation was widespread among the young people. For example, Ria expressed the opinion that the school, the teachers and their racist attitudes were responsible for her exclusion:

> Education got me angry . . . one of my teachers got me angry because she was discriminating against me. I hated that school. I was sick of that teacher picking on me all the time, trying to make me get undressed in front of the boys and all that. She was racist. (Ria)

Ruby acknowledged that she had some responsibility for the exclusion but also considered that the school, teachers and her peer group had contributed:

> I blame myself . . . but mostly the teacher too. I could have hung round with a different crowd. Hung around with somebody else, but I suppose I've just got myself in the wrong crowd. Nowt I could do to get out of it. Same as my friends. (Ruby)

> There were black kids that was posh and popular. They weren't stuck up. They was posh and they knew they was posh. But they weren't stuck up like all the other kids that were posh. [But] I wouldn't hang around with them anyway. They were not popular. They didn't know people in that class so they might just as well sit on their own in it. They sit down on their own and may learn. We know everyone in the class we're just chatting away. Not with the posh coz I never liked any of em. (Ruby)

In her recognition of the potential role that her friendship group appeared to have played in drawing her away from formal education, Ruby highlights the critical importance of her friends for her sense of belonging, providing a source of enjoyment, fun, power and status. Since her friends are critically important to her and her sense of identity, she refuses to forgo her relationship with them, even for academic success. Her need to belong takes precedence over all other considerations. In this sense the oppositional student culture held a powerful claim over the social identities developed by young people in and towards schooling. However, with her school days behind her, Ruby observes with a sense of sadness how she was caught between differing discourses of what constitutes the 'ideal student' (Becker, 1952). An example of this is Ruby's throwaway comment earlier that there was 'Now't I could do to get out of it'. Significantly for the focus of our research it would appear that for Ruby inclusion in the formal life of the school meant effective exclusion from informal friendship groups. Ruby's seductive attachment to her peer group to the detriment of participating in inclusive school activities resonates with the findings of Fordham's (1996) study in the US and the work of Sewell (1997) in the UK. In the former, Fordham posits that academically successful students adopted a strategy of racelessness. Similarly, Sewell (1997) argued that in order to succeed, aspiring black youth had to also assume a form of racelessness and lose their community and black identity to avoid the displeasure of their teachers.

From young people's narratives the influence of peer groups was particularly strong in overcoming and tackling their exclusion and marginalisation and encouraging inclusive activities for example, re-engaging in education. Indeed, Patricia Hill Collins (1990) asserts that mutual respect is pivotal to black people's empowerment. The young people emphasised that their families, friends, communities, social workers and educational and religious groups were instrumental in reclaiming respect and self-love. Respondents stated that friends reinforced their self-worth, reputations and sense of well-being.

In the following extracts the young people explain the photographs (see the Introduction for details of the use of photographs as a component of the fieldwork) of their friends or posse and the role that their friendships played during periods of exclusion and perceived helplessness. The sense they sought to convey, particularly, to each other was that of support.

> So here are you two together with your friend in the photograph, tell me about her. (Researcher)

> That Cherl . . . she was excluded too. (Ruth)

> If my car was going to blow up she'd jump in with me. We were talking about that the other day. We was on about if we was in a car crash and I was driving and we crashed and I couldn't get out and them two could and the car was just about to blow up and them two knew it was going to blow up, would they jump in and die with me or just let me blow up on me own? They both said they'd jump in and die with me. (Ruby)

Got loads of friends but us three like stand out in the crowd. Always together, every day. (Ruby)

Photographs of these relationships also prompted discussions of the strength of feelings associated with the support these relationships have provided. For Desiree, her friend Ria becomes

like a boyfriend, kind of thing. Know what I mean? Coz you're with her all the time, she's protective over you. So she sees you with someone else she'll go mad and then she automatically thinks you are talking about her. (Desiree)

My friends have been there for me one time or another . . . when I was excluded . . . when I needed support or someone to talk to. (Jason)

Similarly

they are just there if I wanted to talk to them. (Keenan)

Indeed, the young people's friends were viewed as offering a uniquely safe place for the excludees. A shared sense of lifestyle, attitudes and experiences had welded the young person into a group that was embodied by a comforting sense of togetherness. The friends offered the excluded young person non-judgemental advice (but only sought by the excluded themselves), sympathy, understanding and a means of escape for the young person from the marginality they were experiencing.

Some of their narratives concerning the significance of friends in helping them overcome school exclusion were similar to those of Alexander's (1996) young black middle-class men whose friendships offered creative responses to discrimination, frustration and recreating resilience in their lives.

Peer Groups, Resistance and Educational (Re)engagement

Friends not only encourage participants to cope with the stress of exclusion but also encourage reinstatement and re-engagement in education. Indeed, friends were perceived to be keenly aware of the black community's uncompromising insistence on high academic performance as a form of resistance to claims of inadequacy in the black self. Thus, friends were found to both actively promote this cultural predisposition towards education and recreate resilience. An example of this is given by Joel:

> I'm the kind of person that as I was excluded I had to kind of bring myself back on the same level terms as the school. I couldn't make them bring me down. They brought me down enough by labelling me and accusing me of doing various things . . . my family, friends and the community knew I could do better. So in that sense, I'm expected to get over it and make something of myself. (Joel)

This comment conveys the mixed discourse of an anti-school attitude with a view that getting on after school required an instrumental engagement with education which accords with Yosso's (2005) notions of aspirational and resistant capital and the significance of education in the 'lifting of the "race"' (Collins, 1990, p. 146).

In this respect, Miranda did not hesitate to act on the advice of her friends to re-engage in education despite having experienced school exclusion:

> They just said 'it was bad that you got kicked out' . . . and . . . were just saying that 'you need to get back into school quick' . . . so I was 'yes', and that's what I did. (Miranda)

At the heart of the narratives of both Joel and Miranda is an illustration of how the peer or friendship groups supported the young people in their attempts to negotiate marginalisation and the consequences it has for self-esteem, identity, aspirations and maintaining a positive orientation to education. In this vein peers and friends work to keep alive the black communities' collective desire for self-knowledge and 'belief in the power of schooling to mitigate racial barriers . . . and make dreams come true' (Fordham, 1996, p. 63).

Summary

This chapter has explored how friendship groups affect the experience of exclusion. The chapter examined the research on the influence of friends and peer groups on black students at school. The black peer group is shown to be a key influence in providing support but the role can be positive and negative. Friends can usurp the importance of academic success because of the need to belong. Overall, peer or friendship groups were seen to be important in helping students to escape from an exclusion identity through the creation of a disposition from which to tackle the effects of exclusion and through providing respect, reinforcing self-worth and encouraging participation in education.

5

COLLECTIVE RESISTANCE

Community Networks and Social Capital in
'Success' Making

Introduction

This chapter demonstrates how community-based organisations and social networks in black communities provide both young people and their families with critical social capital during the transitional phase which helps them overcome their adverse circumstances. Examples are given of the young people's reintegration into mainstream education through advocacy, career advice and assistance in building a collective racial and cultural identity. In essence, community-based organisations functioned to generate a sense of inclusion.

Community, Diasporic Collectives and Social Actions

> Cultural action is always a systematic and deliberate form of action which operates upon the social structure, either with the objective of preserving that structure or of transforming it. As a form of deliberate and systematic action, all cultural action has its theory which determines its ends and thereby defines its methods. (Freire, 1972, p. 46)

This quotation captures one of the significant developments within black diasporic communities, namely the way in which they strive to transform conditions in their communities and the role of social capital in black communities.

The notion of community in general terms is a group of people living together bound by a set of reciprocal relationships. These relationships could include determinants such as spatial, beliefs or economic forces. The concept of community usually assumes some cohesion and harmonious relationships (Alperson, 2002). However, this is problematic if we observe divisions and conflicts on the basis of 'race', gender or social class (Wetherell et al, 2007). Can the notion of community accommodate diversity? Community notions also become problematic if they conflict with individual rights: the extent to which social good is created by community values may be oppressive for groups of individuals such as women or black people. Likewise conceptions of community may mask racism within communities. How does the notion or concept of community destroy or enhance groups or individual identities? Are communities made by exclusions rather than arising from joint norms and values?

In essence, community requires bonds that link people and differences that divide them as the notion of community can function as a strong symbol of those it includes and excludes. The presence of large numbers of black people in Britain has given rise to the notion of the black community but this may be largely 'imagined' rather than tangible (Anderson, 1983). One marker of such a community is the black community organisation. The notion of the community may be imagined within the mind of each black person but in different ways, therefore the relationship of each black individual to the black community is multi-faceted.

Within our study when asked to nominate individuals who had been significant to them during their transitional period around their school exclusion, nearly all of the young people interviewed mentioned the importance of support from community organisations for example:

> the ISSP, they giving me help as well . . . they like keeping me off the streets like . . . like more constructive things to do like more positive things on my mind. (Leon)

and

> [the Director of CEN] would give me advice on what to do, and I do it . . . CEN is very helpful, you need an organisation like CEN . . . [the Director of CEN] has more experience and more knowledge, so it's not something I could have really done on my own. (Mother of Tamara)

The importance of social networks is widely recognised and disadvantaged groups can be further disadvantaged by being unable to access the social networks available to those more advantaged (Perri 6, 1997). This is the explanation put forward by William Julius Wilson when describing ghettos in the US. They are socially isolated from the rest of the network fabric that makes up America and few people have friends outside it or friends unlike themselves. What is important is contact with people outside the ghetto who can act as role models to enable exit from poverty. The importance of contacts outside the family was emphasised by Granovetter (1973) who demonstrated that the most valuable contacts are not the ones with whom people have strong ties, such as kin and neighbours, but those with whom they have weak ties, for example friends of friends.

As outlined in the previous chapters, the literature on black people, education and exclusion demonstrates that there is a long successful tradition of community-led initiatives that are involved in shaping the transitional experience of young black people (Weekes and Wright, 1998; Rhamie and Hallam, 2002). These initiatives are a response to an education system that represents young black people as underachievers and as having anti-education attitudes (Mirza and Reay, 2000). The initiatives are also seen as a response to the victimising and pathologising discourses that sustain the ongoing racial discrimination and exclusion faced by members of the black community (Majors, 2001). Indeed, such views about a racist education system and stereotypical views about young black people was something that was repeatedly commented upon by both the interviewed young excluded people themselves and their families:

> Yeh to me I see that my school is against me that's how I think yeh, that anything I do in school like they bang down on it that's how I see it and cos I'm black as well they just think ah that's just another black naughty kid. (Melona)

and

> 'race' does play a part because I just feel that the system, you know, that they fail the black children . . . they're being ignored and the teachers have low expectations of them. (Mother of Lucinda)

These statements demonstrate the centrality of social capital and cultural capital to the black community's network of co-operation and reciprocity, civic engagement and strong community identity (Bourdieu, 1986; Putnam, 1995). For example, initiatives such as supplementary schools and community mentoring programmes help to enhance young people's self respect and self-discipline. They also inspire young people to have high aspirations to succeed academically and provide them with the opportunity to do so through for example an alternative site of education (Reay and Mirza, 1997; Dove, 1998). There are also community-run mentoring programmes run by and for the black community, which help young people to build or rebuild a confident self-identity and assist in the planning of educational and successful career goals (Weekes and Wright, 1998; Appiah, 2001). In this way black communities engaged in strategies and social action orientated approaches in striving for models of success. These community-led initiatives not only reflect notions of self-help and empowerment but they also provide members with support and advocacy (Christian, 1998).

Nature of the Organisations

Although interviewees mentioned 15 community-based agencies and organisations across London and Nottingham that supported them either during their exclusion or afterwards, two organisations in London and five in Nottingham were found to have played significant roles. These were:

- Intensive Supervision Surveillance Programme (ISSP), London funded through grants from the Youth Justice Board
- Community Empowerment Network (CEN), London
- Take-One Music Studio, Nottingham
- Team Libra, Nottingham
- Build, Nottingham
- Black Families in Education Group, Nottingham
- Positive Action Training and Recruitment Agency (PATRA), Nottingham

For some, funding was more secure than for others but for the majority funding was intermittent and unreliable. Although the agencies varied considerably in their remit, they were all very similar in the type of support they offered to black young people who had been excluded from school. This included practical help such as providing alternative learning sites, advocacy and representation, assistance with reintegration into mainstream education, careers advice and employment guidance as well as emotional support to improve family relationships and help the development of a positive identity. As one mother said:

> I came to see [the Director of CEN] and he advised me and we, umm, we appealed and we had a hearing at the school . . . at least we made our points clear about the way they handled the case was unfair . . . [the Director of CEN] was very good, very supportive . . . he went according to the DfES guidelines, yeh, he was very good, and he was able to point to certain points that they missed and things like that. (Mother of Lucinda)

Not all had been set up to manage school exclusion but had become involved through supporting black families or young people.

Exclusion as a By-product of a Racist System

Exclusion was not a surprising outcome for many workers given an education system they held was still characterised by racist and discriminatory stereotypes:

> The fact of the matter is the schools try and locate the problem, either inherently in the child because you can't do this or you can't do that, or you don't want to do this or that, or in the family, single-parent family, you think how many single-parent families there are, most of whom we deal with, when you survive with distinction and dignity, with power and all these things, struggling against the odds . . . and two, if you're black and a single-parent family. There's something really wrong altogether. And it's the stereotyping, its learning only prejudice and bias and myth from history. (Director, CEN, London)

They acknowledged the damaging effects of these stereotypes on the young person's confidence, self-awareness, identity development and opportunity for a fair education. The work undertaken by the organisations was viewed by its workers as a response to a discriminatory education system:

> education wise teachers need to be alert and, trained is the wrong word, they need to know that different cultures mean that different people will behave differently. Just because a young black child may express himself with his hands or may be coming from a different culture totally doesn't mean that he's going to be aggressive. I don't think young black children are encouraged enough. I don't think they are told that, even if their work is not as good as the average white child, I don't think they are told that their work is good. We need to constantly be telling children that their work is good. If we don't they won't get better. For example, yesterday I was in an assembly in a school and I noticed that the teachers were giving, they give out stickers to people that are sitting nicely. I noticed they were giving the children stickers. The children that were sitting like this, really nicely, sitting straight up with the finger on their lips they were giving them stickers. I noticed a young black child that I've worked with previously he was sitting down, he didn't say a word to nobody throughout the whole assembly, I've seen this happen in the same school with the same child before, he didn't say nothing. He is sitting there quietly, listening, observing everything, but because he wasn't sitting up straight with his hands on his lips he's not been recognised. I was asked to give a child a sticker or a teddy bear to hold and I gave it to that child. The response was quite funny, 'oh he's getting a sticker, why?' He hasn't got behavioural difficulties at all. He is just speaking his mind. If he doesn't like something he'll tell you. He is only nine years old. That's how his parents have empowered him. He will not sit up straight with his hands on his lips, its not the way he's been brought up, he won't do that. Black children need to be encouraged. Black teachers need to understand black children. (Senior Coordinator, Build, Nottingham)

Similarly, another worker had talked about the teachers' stereotyping of black children into sporting roles:

> there is the fact that lots of young black people grow quite tall quite quickly and by some teachers and by other pupils are often perceived as being menacing because black people, because of racism in the past, have

gone into things like sports and everything else and they go into some of the aggressive sports, like American football, boxing. And there's this perception that you know all black people are good fighters. So already you've got this fear factor that grows up around them. And then you've got this other thing where we black people, black males in particular, are supposed to be fighting our war with the sperm. (Team Manager, Team Libra, Nottingham)

The Marginalisation that Results from Exclusion

Due to their knowledge and experience, the organisations and workers had been able to recognise quickly the immediate damage of the school exclusion, as well as the likely long-term effects that would follow. An accumulation of the denial of suitable education, the stigmatisation of being labelled problematic and untrustworthy and the reduced social contact with school friends, which result from being excluded from school combine to create the wider social alienation of many young people who have been excluded from school (Melrose et al, 1999 in Harris and Eden, 2000). Indeed, in terms of the immediate effects, the workers had found that the school exclusion often isolated the young person:

> the big problem with exclusions is of course by its very nature, by the way it works, you're made to feel that you are alone and an isolated case, there's nobody else like you. (Director, CEN, London)

Echoing reports from parents described in Chapter 3, members of the community organisations reported that the exclusion had also affected the relationships, not only between the young person and their parent, but also between the young person and others in their immediate environment:

> They don't feel part of that community. They're not recognised in that community. They are looked on as the thorn in the side in the community. You need to embrace those young people to become the next generation of young people that are going to be mothers and fathers of tomorrow. (Youth Advocate Manager, ISSP, Nottingham)

Being in 'educational limbo' not only affected the young person's immediate educational attainment, but it also affected their long-term employability status, reputation and future prospects. For example, a worrying effect of the school exclusion for some of the young people was an introduction into, or an increase in, offending behaviour. It has been found that young people who have been excluded from school are more likely than non-excludees to offend (Graham and Bowling, 1995; Edmunds, 2000). Some argue that this can be explained by self-fulfilling prophecy, in that the excludee internalises the negative labels about them, as challenging and aggressive troublemakers (Taylor, 1981; Mirza, 1992; Weekes and Wright, 1998), or as 'folk devils' (Cohen, 1980) which then pushes them into anti-social behaviour and further exclusion (Harris and Eden, 2000). This was echoed by one interviewee:

> many of those people excluded from school have been excluded from school a number of months, in some cases out of school a year or even maybe 18 months. They have many hours on their hands and they offend with other young people . . . so you have a lot of these young people at the time that no one has given them direction to do nothing. For that, in terms of the criminal behaviour, we are talking about most of the things they would be known for is street robbery, burglaries. They are the kind of main ones that most of these young men will go to court for, and because of that right, you will find that the problem we have that the education system does not want to work with them no further. (Youth Advocate Manager, ISSP, Nottingham)

Similarly, the Senior Youth Worker for Team Libra (Nottingham) had also talked about the links between exclusion and crime. In addition though he had discussed the role of drugs:

> I think there is a link between exclusion, crime and drugs. Obviously once those students, their confidence has gone, their esteem has gone, and they are not motivated any more, so what are the options for them? They get into drugs . . . they have low self-esteem. Lacked motivation, lacked pride, lacked desire, lacked forward movement to get into college or to get a job. It was easier to run around the streets, perhaps sell drugs. (Senior Youth Worker, Team Libra, Nottingham)

Developing Political Consciousness

Being excluded had also been, for the young people in particular, an alarming realisation of the racist and discriminatory processes that they are likely to experience in wider society (Melrose et al, 1999 in Harris and Eden, 2000; Wright et al, 2000). This had been recognised by the workers:

> racism is within the education system, it's within the housing system, it's within the job market, it's everywhere. What I'm saying is that for these young people . . . is the recognition and ability to sort of logically think through this and things are just starting to drop into place. So these things could have been happening to them earlier, but because they were more child-like, because they were more innocent if I can put it that way, maybe it didn't affect them so much. So for me part of the drop in their achievements and attainments is the fact that they are also beginning to feel the extra burdens of racism. (Team Manager, Team Libra, Nottingham)

The realisation of this was felt to be essential before the workers were able to work with them and assist with their coping of the realisation, by teaching them how to avoid internalising the negative effects of racism:

> I think Rose is a good example, because her mother, she (Rose) is mixed parentage as you know, her mother had the attitude that colour wasn't important. So whatever has happened is more about behaviour. Once she had a mentor who said to her, well look colour is important, you are a black woman and this is how you will be seen, this is how you will be perceived, and raised her awareness of that. Her behaviour then changed . . . Acceptance has got to be taken on board. Never mind how you'd like to be seen. Utopia is a lovely place and that's what we are all working towards. But this is reality, this is the system you are working in and with and this is how you are going to be perceived whether you like it or not. You can't hide the colour you are . . . Therefore once you accept this and who I am. Not being accepted in one camp or another camp, once you've placed yourself you can locate yourself can't you. Then you can find a direction, and sit down and accept the fact, it is racism. It made the difference. Helped her transform herself from the person she was and

being more accepting. I think it's very important. (Senior Community Development Officer, Black Families in Education Group, Nottingham)

Developing a Positive Identity

The exclusion had also impinged on the young people's self-worth and identity development:

> what we observed was in more cases than not, they'd been damaged academically. Their esteem had gone. Their confidence had gone. They didn't think they could achieve any more once they were excluded . . . so the ambition had gone, or had been taken from them if they were permanently excluded. (Senior Youth Worker, Team Libra, Nottingham)

The organisations saw their role as increasing the confidence and self-esteem of the young people:

> I think that most of the work we do is really around boosting their confidence and self-esteem. What we find quite often is that the people who are more likely to be at risk of exclusion are very bright young people. That is the problem. Maybe there's not an appropriate outlet for them to express themselves. They may feel, or it may be reality that they are being stereotyped and pushed in a certain direction whereas they are much more ambitious and that leads to frustration. (Chief Executive, Build, Nottingham)

In Mirza and Reay's terms the organisations are 'new social movements' (2000, p. 524) and are assisting in the construction of an identity designed to counter the impact of oppression. The workers also treated the young people as equals, promoting respect (Collins, 1990) and encouraging them to understand their experiences:

> What we want to do is to work in partnership with young people. We believe in empowering those young people so that they are not, as it were, supplicants, they come to us on an equal basis and they're the ones who know the problem at the sharp end, better than anybody else, better than the teacher, better than the parents, better than I can so they come to me with those problems. And what we show for them I suppose more than anything is (1) the respect and (2) an understanding for their experiences. (Director, CEN, London)

This benefit of this approach on self-esteem and identity development was illustrated by the case of Calvin:

> Now, I mean Calvin been through a lot, with the deaths of some young people that he knew and in his family. In Nottingham, major deaths like —, — was a good friend of Calvin . . . Then the death of [his brother] as well. He's been through a lot . . . but I've seen him grow from a boy to a man to be honest in those two years, physically and mentally, he's become much taller and mentally he can communicate better with people. (Senior Coordinator, Build, Nottingham)

A variety of methods for working with the young people had been adopted by the organisations and workers. These had depended upon whether the organisation was an advocacy, mentoring or support group for example. However, all the organisations had in their approaches provided a service that was based on mutual trust, respect and responsibility:

> these are youths, they're bad, yeah? They are bad. But due to them having such an input, it was theirs that we was building. So they wasn't coming to me and robbing because basically I was saying that if you're robbing from me, you're robbing from yourself because this is ours, we built this. So I was kind of classed as, I don't know, I keep getting these things where people put these banners on me where, because I was working with these bad kids from —, you know what I mean, young West Indian black kids excluded from school and all that type of stuff that they say, they was all coming down there because of the music and the studio. And I allowed them to have an input and showed them a level of respect and trust that they just basically felt comfortable with. And I was basically, I was finding that they was taking, basically, they would come to me with anything, family problems, anything. So, it was like, they was putting me on a pedestal where I didn't realise at first, where, I was looked at, it was kind of weird because I just see myself as a music man really, and now I was getting another banner of something I didn't really intend to do. But just through always trying to help people basically. (Manager, Take-One, Nottingham)

The workers found that such respect, trust and encouragement had positive effects:

Once they realise that someone actually believes what you say and can see where you are being chastised unfairly a lot of them do calm down and their anger goes. They turn into quite good people. (Senior Community Development Officer, Black Families in Education Group, Nottingham)

and

[we say to the young people] 'you can go down that road or you can go down that road', you always given them the choice and they always make the right choice. (Director, CEN, London)

Coping strategies were also seen as an important part of empowerment:

We found it really frustrating because a lot of what we found in the work we did in terms of exclusions was that black boys were experiencing a lot of racism in school and, as we all know, racism does exist in schools. And I think one particular part of our role was to help them channel issues of aggression, frustration into something positive. So for example, we would ask them to make notes and when things happened we'd get them to write it down . . . we do know the majority of the work concentrated on the other things, i.e. they were experiencing a lot of prejudice, a lot of you know being subject to preconceived ideas and stereotypes so they would install that with the view of controlling the pressure at times if you like. (Senior Youth Worker, Team Libra, Nottingham)

In enabling the young people to replace the threatening images held of them (Sewell, 1997), the organisations had encouraged the young people themselves to take an active role:

we've been asked to try and reduce offending by 5% . . . we go about that by young people attending what we call 'life skills sessions' but we are calling the shots . . . which is young people turning up on Thursday afternoons as part of the skills of addressing offending behaviour and we do like workshops, we'll bring in visitors, we'll bring in guest speakers to try and actually address empowerment with those young people, and it's very powerful stuff because the young people are able to talk about where they are in their lives, why they offend, what do they get out of offend-ing, what kind of factors have gone on in their family background, the education, why they feel they are not getting a fair education . . . by doing so, we don't actually talk at the young people, we get the young people to contribute. (Youth Advocate Manager, ISSP, London)

Similarly, in specifically talking about violent crime, another worker had highlighted methods used to lead to life-saving improvements in attitude:

We also have a 'youth forum' where the youth are totally empowered, they are actually running it. One of the things we did last year, November just gone, we did a conference about guns, knives and violence, about stopping it. It was really successful. We had some young people from Birmingham come down and do some talk. We had, I don't know if you've seen the posters outside, of Young, Gifted and Dead, the young black man lying on the floor. We saw it in the newspapers so we phoned up the people who made that poster and it's a lady from Government Office and she had the idea for those posters in, I think it was — in London where the gun crime is rocketed up. She came down and supported us. We had people from the City Council. We had in the daytime a panel of people talking from Pastors of churches to community workers, to teachers and we had people in the audience asking questions. Then in the afternoon we had a group of young people from all over the West Midlands come and entertain, do songs, rap, garage music, dances. (Senior Coordinator, Build, Nottingham)

The workers also encouraged the young people to improve their relationships with other people, especially with authority figures:

We will actually then run a series of things where we will look at things like relationships of the young people. So the relations that we will explore with the young people are relationships between them and their parents. Relationships between them and perceived authority figures, like teachers or the police or anything else. Relationships between the young people and their peers, because we often have this sort of area of what it is that some young people are doing is that they want to do these things just to impress their peers and that can lead on to other things. We look at issues around identity, you know. (Team Manager, Team Libra, Nottingham)

Reintegration into Education and Enhancing Employability

All the workers had recognised the problem of reintegration difficulties for black excludees, especially for those who also have offended:

> The difference is that when people see your black skin to begin with you are already being marked down if you like on a scenario. What then happens is that unfortunately, I'll go back to the thing with the identity cards, we already have systems in this country that penalise black people. We know that, there's no two ways about it. The problem we've got is that if a black person has a criminal record as well that further disadvantages them. (Team Manager, Team Libra, Nottingham)

As such they had all sought to reintegrate the young person back into mainstream education and enhance their employability status. They had not only done so by providing information, advice and support for the young people, but also by actually training them and equipping them with employable skills:

> the support that we have, good contact with different bodies to support those young people beyond being excluded from the school process, but being able to skill and train them, so that they can become employable. (Youth Advocate Manager, ISSP, London)

Providing activities in which the young people could get involved was seen as supporting re-entry into mainstream education but there was also a recognition that sometimes alternatives to mainstream education had to be found:

> we try and keep their minds occupied, so when they do get back into school they've got something to look forward to when they come out of school and they can go to youth clubs and things like that. We've tried to also help them with the alternative provision, direct them in the right place. (Youth Worker, Team Libra, Nottingham)

Many of the organisations had also provided the young people with contacts. For example, PATRA organised conferences in which the young people could learn about the education and employment options available to them:

We've managed to develop over the last six years, a youth convention. We've got employers coming here, setting up stalls, not only employers but also colleges and armed forces, to give advice and support young people coming to the end of their school days and don't want to go into further education . . . to let them realise what is available within employment under the modern apprenticeship training programme, and also what support there is for people who, after being kicked out of school for a given period and if they would like to come back into the education system to further their education, to be able to let them identify what sort of support there is within the education system, within the employment structure, within the armed forces in order to get them back. Get them to be employable or make a life for themselves. (Chief Executive, PATRA, Nottingham)

The Community as an Important Learning Site

I . . . prefer studying in the community and I find a lot of other people do too. (Manager, Take-One, Nottingham)

There is an emerging body of research on community organisations as alternative 'learning sites' (Craig, 2000; Department for Education and Skills, 2003). These studies, particularly, in relation to disaffected young people, highlight the roles of alternative practices, such as mentoring and networking in the way young people gain knowledge and expertise from their peers and from significant adults within those community contexts. Indeed, studies indicate that black young people experiencing difficulties at school have often benefited greatly from out-of-school-hours learning in community-run initiatives such as supplementary schools, mentoring projects, music-based projects (Department for Education and Skills, 2003).

The Chief Executive of PATRA, Nottingham, explained:

some of the children, because of their experiences within the classroom do not want to go back into the school.

The Development Worker from Black Families in Education Group, Nottingham, had expanded upon the reasons for this:

[excludees] feel that the education system has let them down . . . a lot of children think 'my education has finished, what's the next move?'

As a consequence of this and mainstream education and statutory provision's inadequate execution of the post-exclusion and reintegration guidelines, the organisations and their workers promoted the black community as an alternative learning site:

> a lot of young people because of it, I mentioned the instilled racism within the education system and a lot of young people because of their experience through instilled racism are more comfortable in working with people from their own kind, within organisations that provide that service. (Chief Executive, PATRA, Nottingham)

For the interviewed workers and their organisations, the community had provided alternative learning in several ways. They identified supplementary schooling, in particular schooling, that focused on African-Caribbean history and culture:

> So for instance —, which is an after-school study club, was started by workers from Team Libra. It's an independent entity but it deals with working with young people, teaching them skills like Swahili, French, and giving them African history in particular. So they get to learn a little bit about their background and they understand that the African person does have a fulfilled sort of history within the overall aims of what this civilisation is. We also work with other groups to try and develop things . . . We sort of like work in a wide area of schools under black Afro-Caribbean specified issues. (Team Manager, Team Libra, Nottingham)

Indeed, one worker had commented on the importance of assisting young African-Caribbeans in this way:

> because it's something that they want to do, they are actually quite focused. (Youth Worker, Team Libra, Nottingham)

Such support also helped to redress the racist type of education that was largely being taught in mainstream education:

> it still is a mono-cultural education system, which is excluding some people. (Team Manager, Team Libra, Nottingham)

One worker had discussed how and why black communities were attempting to redress this racism:

I think what the black communities are looking for is change, transformation, new opportunities because people share a vision and that is most important. What's our vision? You know legacies of loss, and what I've been trying to work out is what is it that our young people remember, sometimes vaguely, because I feel that the problem with formal education very often is it destroys your rootedness and your sense of belonging to your family, relationship with parents and siblings as well as a relationship history. (Director, CEN, London)

Another type of alternative learning was holding more creative programmes, workshops and training courses that were designed around the young people's interests, for example, music, dance and drama:

We also do other initiatives which is like accreditation courses for young people, which is like the bowl of weightlifting qualification, the pool lifeguard qualification, first aid qualifications. We are also working on accreditation on music workshop, issues you know young people express interest in music. We have initiatives we are doing, barbering accreditation . . . hair and beauty . . . basically what we try and do really is just kind of look on what would be the norm for young people in an education context of what they view they would like to achieve and how do we qualify them to turn the system, to be able to get on. (Youth Advocate Manager, ISSP, London)

These special interest programmes were not only designed to provide the young people with their own space and to stimulate them, but also to give them 'that push start' (Youth Worker, Team Libra, Nottingham) by enabling them to use their interests and skills to enhance their future prospects:

the community studio is primarily like a drop-in space but it's there to use music as a tool, to develop young people's capacity to learn, to become professionals in their own right, to become leaders, to have responsibility. So we do that through workshops. We do that through training, which is linked to the colleges. We do that by giving people the space and time to be able to create their own music and collaborate with other people in the community. (Community Development Officer, Take-One, Nottingham)

In addition to these roles, the organisations also provided the young people with 'life education', in particular the education about issues with which young black people are stereotypically associated, i.e. drugs, sexuality, sexual health and teenage parenthood:

> Other things that we look at is socially, where are young people going to be going once they leave school? What are their aspirations? Do they understand that they need an educational basis to build on if they want to be seen as successful within the sort of society we live in, or even in the community that we're living in. We also talk about issues around sexuality. Quite often it's mainly young males we are dealing with so we talk about issues around teenage pregnancy and the responsibility that they as males should have to their partners, to their children if they go down that road . . . Also we do work around areas of sexual health and everything with young women as well, when it's necessary. Because its not just a single-sex activity. We do quite a lot of work around drugs because our community is often given the title of the people that are, if you like, supplying the drugs to the whole of this country. I mean the fact that the country itself seems to be a drug-consuming nation is beyond me. Its not as if black people suddenly came into this country and started giving these things out left, right and centre. (Team Manager, Team Libra, Nottingham)

Providing Alternative Sources of Support

> Any gaps in society, try and help plug those. (Community development officer, Nottingham)

A large part of assisting the young people and their families overcome the exclusion was through empowerment. The workers did this by attempting to provide the opportunities denied to them by mainstream education:

> I just have a team that is trying to support the young people for what they have been supposed to get and have been denied of, and try to do the best we can do within the parameters and move the boundaries and knock the door hard and move the doors off the hinges to make changes. (Youth Advocate Manager, ISSP, London)

It was also seen as a response to the vacuum created by the shortcomings of statutory service provision and the lack of support they provided for young people and families:

> Sometimes they phone you late at night because that's the time when they've managed to screw up enough courage to do so . . . what's happening in the mainstream, what's happening in the schools, what's happening in the local authority, because I find sometimes that the response that they get [from them] is quite arrogant, you know 'how dare you bother me, don't you know I'm busy' whereas my response is 'we're never too busy'. (Director, CEN, London)

The importance of being accessible was emphasised by this worker:

> Also a lot of the work we do tends to be not within work time, because you are working, you've got your job, but really those supporting people can be called at 11 o'clock at night. (Senior Community Development Officer, Nottingham)

They could spend long hours working, often on a voluntary basis, on the exclusion cases:

> from say nine o'clock in the morning until ten to eleven o'clock at night. And that's five, six, seven days a week. (Youth Advocate Manager, ISSP, London)

Types of negative responses reported by parents of excluded children were similarly highlighted:

> Parents will actually contact us and say 'I've had this letter from the school, I don't really understand what its all about, I've tried to talk to the school, the school are just accusing me of being stroppy, obnoxious, sort of like blocking the way of progress and that's not really the case. Will you come down and support us in this thing?' So we get parents that will do that because obviously a lot of parents feel that because they're Afro-Caribbean that they are actually seen as people who shouldn't be in this country and shouldn't be getting any services. And quite often they just feel that they are being picked on as well as their children are being picked on. So they want support from people, or from organisations, that they feel know what they are doing and can actually help on that side. (Team Manager, Team Libra, Nottingham)

The fact that the services they provided were often struggling for funding sometimes caused additional anger:

all we want is quality of life. I don't believe black people should do it for free. We done it free in the early days, slavery. Ain't doing shit for free. (Youth Advocate Manager, ISSP, London)

The Importance of Working with Families

The detrimental effects caused by exclusion from a school also extend to the excludee's family (Cohen and Hughes, 1994 quoted in Parsons, 1999; Parsons et al, 1996; Pomeroy, 2000). Such damaging effects were acknowledged, in particular the feelings of powerlessness that many parents of excluded children often report:

We work from a parent's perspective: where the parent feels in control of their own child. Because they will go to one meeting and Social Services tell them, we are working with the child that way, the police are doing it this way, schools doing it another way. But the parent had no say in the whole process. Just feel they are being carried along. So we decided to get something together where the parents have to be consulted and they have a right to say, 'this is how I want to participate and my child in whatever your organisations are doing'. Just to give parents back some control. (Senior Community Development Officer, Black Families in Education Group, Nottingham)

The excludee's family has largely been found to be a valuable support network in helping young people to overcome their exclusion (Pomeroy, 2000). The interviewed workers had recognised the important role that family members played in supporting their children with the exclusion process:

because parents like to support each other in the community, they talk to each other and people tell them about what resources are available for them . . . so they can support their child. (Development Worker, Black Families in Education Group, Nottingham)

Hence, a large part of assisting the young people with the exclusion had been done through improving and utilising family relations:

They (young person) come in angry and of course the parent wants to make a good impression, 'I'm terribly sorry' and they apologise. Our immediate response is 'don't apologise for your child, if they were not angry there would be something wrong with her or with him and you've got to understand that . . .' However, we say to them 'we don't want to be taken by surprise' and sometimes this leads to an interesting development. The child will say 'well I better tell you this then', the mother sniffs and says 'but you didn't tell me that' . . . So what we do then is to use that as a learning opportunity and to say well 'ok, why is it that she or he didn't tell you that, isn't it because you'd react in the same way you're reacting now' so when we meet it's a learning opportunity for all of us, for the parent, for the child, for myself. (Director, CEN, London)

Many of the organisations saw a longer-term solution in empowering and informing parents:

It's about building parents as well. You need to give them awareness. Most people have two or three children. So if the eldest child is having problems at some point the younger one may experience something. Just the fact they have the same family name, going through the same school. So if you can empower that parent to deal with the situation they can protect the second child and the third child . . . so we look at the situation and try to encourage parents. (Senior Community Development Officer, Black Families in Education Group, Nottingham)

These sentiments are an example of one of the factors identified by Rhamie and Hallam's (2002) examination of the factors contributing to success among African-Caribbean professionals in the UK. They pointed to the importance of the family and community working together to create a 'sense of belonging' and acceptance and foster achievement and success, which compensate for low expectations and resources in the school.

Shared Experiences

In addition to their training and knowledge, all the workers within organisations felt they understood the excludees' experience, in some cases because they themselves had been excluded:

It's kind of weird because Take-One came about from my kind of travels through getting back on the straight and narrow, are you with me? Cos, I was like unemployed and not at school, and left with no qualifications and all that type of stuff. So, basically, I started off in my music career. (Manager, Take-One, Nottingham)

Hence, their work was largely driven by genuine passion, a desire to assist and support the young people and their families, and a need to empower them as members of the black community:

I have a commitment to the work and desire to it. I enjoy doing what I'm doing, the reason I enjoy doing what I'm doing is because it is about young black men, and young black women as well. (Youth Advocate Manager, ISSP, London)

Often the support was localised and personalised more deeply because the worker lived in the community:

I live round where they live. (Manager, Take-One, Nottingham)

However, workers were keen to emphasise that having a sense of shared experience with the young people, did not mean that they were not fair or rigorous in dealing with cases:

The other thing is that we are not in any way sloppy about what we do. We're very rigorous in interrogating the situation, we want to know what happened and we want to know why has it escalated to this point, what did you do that escalated it or what could you have done that would have defused the situation? So by the time we've gone through the first telephone call, the interview, the hearings and then the reintegration, they will have gone through an experience that actually develops them with a sense of responsibility as well as a sense, not only of their own rights, but the rights of others as well. (Director, CEN, London)

Similarly, one worker had emphasised the fairness of such an approach:

We don't want to wrap our young black people up in cotton wool. When a young black person comes through our door and says 'I've been excluded' and this and that, we'll say 'ok. How might you have contributed to this?' (Chief Executive, Build, Nottingham)

Working for the empowerment of black individuals and successfully assisting the young people overcome their exclusion clearly gave the workers job satisfaction:

> I would say, too right, it is the most fulfilling, satisfying, challenging job I've done up to now, simply because I'm allowed to create something that's allowed to be innovative . . . I make contacts with all those relevant agencies but pull the strengths together with my support team to be able to support those young people. (Youth Advocate Manager, ISSP, London)

and

> I'm grateful for my job, I love my job, I have to be forced to take holidays. It's that bad. I mean, I constantly lose my holidays cos I never take them. (Manager, Take-One, Nottingham)

Their enthusiasm and dedication were reflected in their success rates:

> when they sometimes years after our first contact, they come back to us and ask for our advice or just touch base or when they phone us, it's amazing what we get out of them in terms of energy and good feeling of good will . . . CEN has a 100% success rate in terms of reintegration, either at the excluding school or the new school where the young person finds admission. (Director, CEN, London)

Support workers clearly valued the relationships that developed between them and the young people they worked with:

> I know I've got a positive impact because when I see them on the street they are like 'oh are you all right?' . . . I'll ask them if they've done the lyrics for the track that they are supposed to be coming down to. I'll ask them if they are still playing football or things like that. Because I've done quite a lot of work with them, I know what kind of things they are into and it's just nice to see them out. When they see me it's like 'oh there's —'. It just puts a smile on my face . . . they know I'm easy to talk to. I mess about with them. I bully them a little, nice bullying, well I'm like 'you come here, what are you doing?' They are all right with me. It's nice. (Youth Worker, Team Libra, Nottingham)

Indeed in some of the organisations, young people who had been successfully helped by the organisation in the past were returning with their own experience and applying to assist the current intake of young people:

> the organisation has aged, in that we're seeing mentees becoming mentors. Which is great. You get a call out of the blue, somebody saying 'I was helped by Build ten or eleven years ago and I'm now employed or studying at university and I'd like to give something back.' So we have had an impact. (Chief Executive, Build, Nottingham)

These findings can be seen as further support for Yosso's (2005) critique of the traditional application of Bourdieu and Passeron's (1977) theory of cultural capital as it is used to explain the lower social and academic outcomes of people of colour. Yosso's position is that, according to cultural capital theory, their lesser social and academic attainment would imply a lack of cultural capital among members of black communities and would also explain any subsequent social mobility. She wishes to move away from a deficit view of 'Communities of Color as places full of cultural poverty disadvantages' (2005, p. 82) and instead focuses on the wealth of cultural knowledge, skills, abilities and contacts possessed by socially marginalised groups that often go unrecognised and unacknowledged. This diverges from the traditional notion of what constitutes capital as held by the white middle classes and only attained through success in an educational system controlled by the white middle-class community.

The findings also undermine the use of deficit models that have previously been used to explain 'underachievement' and the lack of social mobility among the black communities. In doing so they echo the work of Sampson et al (1999) and Akom (2003) who proposed the notions of 'community social capital' and 'critical social capital', respectively, as the means by which black communities respond to issues affecting the community. Critical social capital departs from traditional notions of social capital by placing a greater focus on the collective dimensions of community change. It also centres on how developing a positive racial and cultural identity and political consciousness provide an important community and social resource for facilitating activities for change. In addition, the essential role played by the black community organisations appears to reflect a traditional means of social organisation which challenges the fashionable postmodern discourses which place the primacy of the consumerist individualism of the late 1990s communitarianism over traditional means of community social action.

Summary

Interviews with members of community organisations that had been identified by the young people as sources of support highlighted several important findings. Having a strong belief that school exclusion would lead to marginalisation, social exclusion and possibly to an involvement in crime and drugs, these community workers saw their role as helping the young people develop a positive identity and reintegration into education and employment. They did this by realising the potential of the community as an alternative learning site, providing alternative sources of support and above all, working with families. These workers were totally committed to helping the young people: some of them had experienced exclusion themselves. They worked long hours often with little chance of continuing funding or resources. Their accounts can be seen as further support for Yosso's (2005) critique of the traditional application of Bourdieu and Passeron's (1977) theory of cultural capital as an explanation of the lower social and academic outcomes of black people. They also undermine the use of deficit models as an explanation of different patterns of achievement and the lack of social mobility in black communities.

6

YOUTH, 'RACE'/ETHNICITY AND SOCIAL MOBILITY IN CONTEMPORARY SOCIETY

Introduction

> I want you to know that we have very much in common. For nothing in my life's path would have predicted that I would be standing here as the first lady of United States of America. There was nothing in my story that would land me here. I wasn't raised with wealth or resources of any social standing to speak of . . . If you want to know the reason why I'm standing here, it's because of education. (Michelle Obama)[1]

This quotation is especially illuminating because Michelle Obama's personal statement suggesting that education is seen as a key to success reflects a narrative of meritocracy and work ethic, which is embedded in black diaspora habitus. This statement also goes to the heart of the liberal democratic meritocratic ideals of education and schooling which is adhered to on both sides of the Atlantic (e.g. Fordham, 1996; Loury et al, 2005).

Our study therefore proffers the chance to reflect critically on current theory on social identities, schooling, education, social mobility and social justice. Furthermore, because the youth phase is significant for social reproduction, a focus on the youth phase 'remains vital to understanding how familiar social class, gender "racial"/ethnic divisions are repopulated, is contested or overcome' (MacDonald et al, 2005, p. 875). Drawing on the analysis from our study the chapter will link these issues to the possible barriers created by school exclusion for successful transitions. Given the key role of education in facilitating social mobility, what does denying access to education through the process of exclusion say about social justice? The involvement of non-mainstream institutions, for example, community-based institutions in counteracting barriers from mainstream institutions to social mobility, offers a fascinating angle on debates concerning transitions and social mobility. This highlights the meanings, implications and caveats in relations to ways in which collective social action (Freire, 1972) can transform structural inequalities.

In this chapter we will discuss some of the themes and issues identified in the previous chapters, in addition to developing ways of understanding the young people's perspective theoretically. Similar to Ball et al (2000), 'We are assembling a conceptual tool-kit with and adding to existing bodies of work' (p. 143).

Social Identities, Social Justice, Schooling and Transitions

As signalled already the educational biographies of our young people have raised issues about the limits and possibilities of current analytical and theoretical approaches in the so-called 'trajectory studies' of how young people make 'transitions' to, are 'propelled' into, or 'navigate' their way towards their adult occupations and identities (e.g Ball et al, 2000; MacDonald and Marsh, 2001). Navigation is probably an apt metaphor given the number of interruptions that our young people have experienced.

Parekh (2000) argues that education is a virtue in all democratic societies and serves as a gateway to employment for all citizens. Alongside social justice and social mobility, education is also seen as essential for encouraging greater social cohesion. Further, Parekh (2000) concludes that the British education system, though designed to meet the needs of its citizens, does not appear to equip a large proportion of young black people with the skills needed to achieve their full potential. Indeed, as already discussed, Gillborn (2008) argues that educational 'race' inequality in the UK, particularly in relation to schooling, is a form of 'locked-in inequality' whereby the schooling system is seen to disadvantage young black females and males in two ways: through school exclusion and inequality of attainment.[2] What is therefore a major issue here is the implication of this form of locked-in inequality for social justice.

This study represents not only a key issue regarding social identities and social justice in education but it links the discourse on the problematic relationship between 'race' and education that has framed UK social democratic policy since the 1960s with contemporary concerns with how young black people's schooling experiences shape their transitions on leaving compulsory education. It is argued that a way of understanding the influence of differential experiences of transition for young black people is to examine the role of education. In particular, how school exclusion affects their life chances and the nature of their transition. Earlier chapters have described the strength of feeling expressed by young people, parents, grandparents and other carers and community organisations regarding this matter in the study. Whilst acknowledging individual failings they also felt structural inequality and racism was significant.

Our work certainly draws attention to the efficacy of policy aimed at fostering equality of opportunity in this area. For instance, recent educational policy approaches concerning achievement of black students have tended to advocate that schools should focus their energies on raising aspirations or providing positive role models rather than for instance, addressing racism and structural inequalities (Archer and Francis, 2007). This could only be done if the education system as a whole engaged in a more concerted way with the complexity of racialised identities and inequality and the ways these interact with gender and social class. The Macpherson Report (Macpherson, 1999) has been important in situating racism and the Race Relations (Amendment) Act (2000) places a duty of care on organisations to eliminate unlawful discrimination and to promote equality of opportunity and good relations between people of different racial groups. Yet the disproportionate numbers of black students being excluded from school in their final years of schooling persists, affecting their life chances. Invariably our data suggest that racism and disadvantage remain potent and detrimental forces within British schools (Archer and Francis, 2007). Thus within the context of transition, the extent to which schooling potentially acts as a brake on social mobility for young black females and males is a problem of great concern to all modern social progressives. In the USA, the underlying achievement gap debate referred to in the introductory chapter, is a fundamental dispute concerning whether or not the USA is a meritocracy. At the heart of this debate lies the question of whether or not schools are themselves meritocratic institutions that reward students based solely on objective measures of ability and egalitarian principles. That is, does the achievement gap signify a lack in the individual (Hernstein and Murray, 1994) or culture (Thernstrom and Thernstrom, 2003) or under-performing groups, or does it imply structural forces that affect certain groups in ways that lead to poor attainments (Ogbu 1974, 1978)? Schooling is at the heart of the American dream (e.g. Fordham, 1996; Loury et al, 2005). However, as Branglinger (2003) points out, 'the classical ideological "American dream of social mobility" combined with tales of "school as meritocracy" cause a range of students to believe that the playing field is level and those who excel do so by virtue of natural talents while those who fail are lacking' (p. 7). As mentioned in the introductory chapter, the educational resources playing field was constructed to create inequality between blacks and whites (e.g Ladson-Billings, 2006) but it would appear to remain unequal to this day (Roza and Hill, 2004; Education Trust, 2006; Ladson-Billings, 2006; Liu, 2006).

Linking Agency, Structure, Young Black People and Social Mobility

The young people did feel that their experience of schooling and exclusion had the potential to adversely circumscribe their life chances. Yet the young people had hope, self-belief and aspirations. The young people regardless of their social class and gender did recognise the importance of education and social mobility and identified with the ideology of meritocracy. Many stayed on longer in education (further and higher education) in order to redress the unsatisfactory outcome of their schooling in terms of educational qualification. The young people expected negative structural experiences but felt that what were needed were strategies to negotiate or navigate structure dominating over agency. The young people's approach has many resonances with that reported by Mirza's (2004) study of young black women who had evolved 'a system of strategic rationalization' (p. 206) as a way of responding to obstacles to accessing educational opportunities.

What was clear from our study was that the young people did not accept the dominant discourse about their potential and appeared to construct their identities in opposition to the dominant discourse which was perceived as having limited prospects. The question is what generates and drives the young people's aspirations? The answer involved several interrelated aspects. First, the aspirational capital in valuing education and personal achievement was constructed in specifically racialised cultural terms and was characterised by notions of 'being somebody', 'lifting the "race"' or more specifically, the black diasporic sentiments of self-advancement. Second, the need to eradicate the stigma of school exclusion heightened motivation for social mobility and 'success'. Third, the importance of education and achievement was recognised by family or other carers and the community. Finally, the young people appeared to have learnt an awareness of the need for social support and collaborative action through their experience of marginality.

Our analysis highlights some issues associated with theorising the individual's strategic response, choice and decision making arising from experiences of living within complex structures of power and inequality, which relate to the concept of 'structured individualism' (Furlong and Cartmel, 1997) mentioned above. We feel that it is important to recognise at this point that aspiration and a desire to succeed cannot by themselves overcome structural inequality. They do not equate with, or translate straightforwardly into, labour market success. So while the young people's aspirations seemed to be having a positive impact on their motivation to succeed and were helping them to make strategic, timely decisions regarding their future, they alone could not guarantee success. Educational success is not directly matched by labour market success as the experiences of many black people show (Cregan, 2002). In the British labour market those in professional or white collar jobs, for example, still encounter unequal pay differentials and the glass ceiling: blocked promotion to senior levels. One of the most prominent black figures in the UK, Trevor Phillips, Chair of the Equality and Human Rights Commission, the public body with a legal duty to encourage better race relations and powers to prosecute offenders, caused a media storm in November 2008 when he claimed in the *Guardian* that a 'British Barack Obama would not have been elected to Prime Minister in this country' (*Guardian*, 2008). This draws attention to how black people are still circumscribed in their choice of employment and how racism and discrimination are barriers towards the integration of black people in the wider labour market.

As with success in education, the participation of black people in the labour market and their choice of employment is not simply a matter of their own efforts, self-determination, resourcefulness and agency. The social mobility of black people is also a matter of barriers in the form of structural constraints. However, in discussing this it must be borne in mind that the meaning of social mobility is disputed. For economists it is primarily a matter of increasing income. For sociologists it is a rise in occupational status. In this study, the most useful definition is that provided by Aldridge (2003, p. 10): 'the movement or opportunities for movement between different social classes or occupational groups'.

Examining social mobility Blanden et al (2005) found that of the eight highly developed countries in their study the UK and USA have the lowest levels of social mobility. The UK has similar levels of social mobility to the USA but the UK position relative to the USA has declined over recent decades. It is suggested that social mobility in the UK has become limited. Blanden et al (2005) reveal a strong correlation between social mobility and income inequality. In other words, countries with larger income differences tend to have lower social mobility. In the later twentieth century social mobility in the USA declined as income differences widened.

Such data suggest that people may not be able to achieve a better social or economic position for themselves and their families by their own merits and hard work. Equality of opportunity essentially means the possibility of social mobility.

Merit, agency and self-determination are important in social mobility but for relatively disadvantaged groups merit-based factors are not sufficient in determining opportunities for social mobility. There are structural constraints involved. The class structure is clearly a significant factor for many sociologists. Goldthorpe (2004) suggests that there is little evidence of changes in social openness in the UK despite a vast investment in education aimed at improving equality of opportunity. In fact, it has been found that there has been downward movement for some groups in the class structure in the UK. Blanden et al (2002, 2004) demonstrate that expansion of higher education in the UK has largely benefited people with richer parents but overall has led to a fall in social mobility.

Heath and McMahon (2005) showed that ethnic minority groups in the UK do less well in terms of social mobility than their white counterparts of the same social class. The assumption has long been held that with schooling, dispersal and assimilation, immigrant groups and their children experience upward mobility. However, the 'race'/ethnic disadvantages of the first generation of black African-Caribbean immigrants are actually less than those facing the second generation. Even then, this upward mobility for the second generation of ethnic minority immigrant groups in the UK has been less than for British-born whites (Heath and McMahon, 2005).

There are few comparative studies of social mobility of the black populations of the UK and USA. Differences in the length of settlement of the black populations and numbers between the two countries make comparison difficult. However, in the USA there are greater opportunities for the black elite to rise than in the UK. This is largely a result of a much larger black population both absolutely and relatively. Sections of the black population in the USA have a political power not present in the UK. This power can be used to gain jobs for black people in the private and public sectors. However, in the UK the black African-Caribbean population has established itself more in the housing market than in the USA (Modood, 2005).

The actual advancement of black people through upward social mobility clearly has structural constraints in terms of income and social class. For the critical race theorists (CRT) the major structural constraint is racism. What is important for CRT are not just individual acts of racism or prejudice but the hidden and subtle operation of white power that leads to black people being disadvantaged (see for example Bell, 1995; Crenshaw et al, 1995; Ladson-Billings and Tate, 1995; West, 1995). CRT regards racism as normal and endemic and something that black people confront every day. In respect of social mobility CRT regards meritocracy largely as a myth with black people being subordinated to white privilege. This results in unearned assets. For example, the main beneficiaries of affirmative action in the USA have been white women. The main beneficiaries of the expansion of higher education in the UK have been members of the white middle class. For CRT social mobility for blacks is tolerated only if it promotes white self-interest.

Clearly a significant structural constraint for upward social mobility of any relatively disadvantaged group is that non-group members can influence their life chances. This can be the case for the black populations in both the UK and the USA. Social and political institutions with the necessary power influence the mobility of 'racially'/ethnically disadvantaged groups. However, this also applies to class and gender. CRT therefore underplays intersectionality, that is where black people are positioned in multiple structures of power by 'race', class and gender.

With this intermeshing of structural constraints on social mobility the question can be asked as to whether aspirant young black people are imbued with a false consciousness or are 'social dupes' (Willis, 1977). Why in the face of these constraints is there still a persistent desire to achieve? In essence, our analysis suggests that some theories of social reproduction and education do not always fit or extend neatly to explain black social mobility.

Social Ties, Community Capital: Transformative Agents

Despite the structural constraints highlighted above there are struggles by communities and families within communities for social advancement of their young black people. The degree of involvement of young people's parents, carers, friends and community organisations in the construction of their aspirations challenges traditional theorising and policy models of aspirations as individualised decisions based upon personal interest and aptitude (Giddens, 1991; Beck, 1992). Instead, aspiration appeared to be a product of complex interpersonal and collective relations and the negotiation of competing demands and desires.

These findings highlight the significance of the family or carer for the young people in our study. Family is significant within all the young people's narratives. A majority of these young people did come from supportive and stable home environments. Families are clearly significant for most of the young people in forming social perspectives and generating resources for identity formation. Moreover, mothers appear to be at the forefront of all this. Further, a majority of the parents and carers were from a second generation migrant background[3] and, accordingly, are imbued with the meritocratic view that ability and effort would bring educational success and consequently improved occupational prospects. There was some ambivalence about their children's exclusion. For instance, parents and carers reported distrust of the education system. They expected the school to deny full educational rights to their children in some way. Yet the majority of parents and carers, particularly the mothers, reacted to their children's involvement in exclusion with a sense of having failed in some way. As expressed by Richard's mother (Chapter 3) 'It is difficult to describe how embarrassed you feel'. As, Reynolds (2005) explains 'a central aspect of [black mothers'] mothering work involves them developing coping strategies that enable their children to cope with and respond to racial discrimination which they, as black children will most inevitably face' (p. 70).

In the terms of Yosso's familiar capital, families played a role in the career or life planning of almost all the young people, except those few without families or whose family life had totally broken down. This is not to overlook the fact that there was variation among families and parents. For instance, there was an important classed dimension to the types of information and resources. Some parents, typically the middle class, are pro-active and interventionary in choices and decisions about post-schooling. Working-class families, particularly those without personal experiences of either further or higher education, were reliant on resources mustered from outside the family in support of their children. For these families the interaction between the home and community provision was crucial for providing the young person with what they needed to succeed in overcoming school exclusion.

Yosso's (2005) argument about community cultural wealth as a means of reinforcing notions of collective rights, responsibilities or obligations that can be mobilised towards collective social action becomes relevant here. It might, for instance, be concluded from our study that the existence of black community provision fostered a sense of collective identity or political consciousness which testifies to a high degree of vested interest and belief in the value of the community, however imagined and in whatever form. Indeed, at its most abstract, the symbol of 'the community' remains a primary and formidable instrument of opposition. In this vein, support within the black community functions as 'bridge ties' that cut across class, gender, occupation and generation (Granovetter, 1973; Goulborne and Solomos, 2003). So community members do benefit from the ties that provide access to advantageous resources which can operate to facilitate mobility goals. Of course, there is the need to recognise that the extent to which community provision can assist in the facilitation of young people's socio-economic advancement will be contingent on formation, locality and the strength of the organisation. For instance, in neighbourhoods with strong social organisation, residents can benefit from multiple social ties which help to alleviate the negative effects of marginalisation. In contrast, in neighbourhoods with weak social organisation, residents may draw on social ties to help with their daily survival, but these local ties are unlikely to provide resources beyond survival needs. In essence, without romanticising their role, black community provision is seen to collectively open up transformative possibilities for their communities. Moreover, they provide young black people with critical resources which consist of intergenerational ties that cultivate expectations and aspiration for upward social advancement. It goes without saying that opportunities in youth and final destinations in adulthood are still strongly influenced by an individual's gender, 'race', ethnicity and social class status, despite the fact that the risks and uncertainties of restructured transitions tend to engender a greater sense of individual autonomy (Furlong and Cartmel, 1997; Green et al, 2001, Mitchell et al, 2001).

Summary

This chapter examined the limits and possibilities for transitions in young black people's lives. The role of education is seen as important in both transitions and transformations of the lives of young people. This raised the issue of education either promoting a meritocracy or denying it through structural constraints.

The young people in the study sought to overcome both structural constraints and the denial of schooling through exclusion. Aspirational values require the overcoming of structural inequalities. Even with educational success, there is no guarantee of success in the labour market. Social mobility was seen to be denied by structural factors of class, gender and 'race'. CRT is particularly sceptical about the possibilities of social mobility for black people.

However, the positive aspirational values of the young black people were seen to challenge traditional theorising. Family and carers were seen to play a significant role in supporting these values. Likewise black community provision was seen to be vital in cultivating expectations for advancement.

7

UNDERSTANDING BLACK YOUTH

'Success' and Transitions in Society Today

Introduction

> Structures shape people's practices, but it is also people's practices that
> constitute (and reproduce) structures . . . if enough people or even a few
> people who are powerful enough to act in innovative ways, their action
> may have the consequence of transforming the very structures that gave
> the capacity to act. (Sewell, 1992, p. 4)

The title of this chapter and the quote by Sewell highlight the focus of
this book, namely, the focus on exploring the journey of young black
people overcoming the impact of disadvantaged compulsory education to achieve success at the 'transitional phase'. In essence, it argues
for a nuanced understanding of young black people's transitional
experiences through the exploration of how dominant discourses
link the intersection of youth, 'race'/ethnicity, gender, social class
and the experiences of compulsory education in the shaping of
inclusionary and exclusory transitions. The chapter also raises the
question of the extent to which the terms of the debate concerning transitional success, exclusion and stratification warrant further
discussion.

Although the basis of the research was educational disadvantage, in
particular, school exclusion, the book was able to provide a commentary on the wider social and political significance of exclusion experienced by the black community and more significantly to examine how
they were able to resist, challenge and overturn negative representations in order to achieve positive and successful outcomes in other

areas. In doing so, the book considers matters of social mobility that are relevant in both the UK and US. Here, critical race theory, the contribution of postcolonial theorists, the black feminist critique, and the work of symbolic interactionists such as Goffman (1963) have been used to argue that, rather than negatively pathologising and problematising the black community, their drive for self-improvement must be considered. This involves examining how social structure, agency, materiality and resources, structural identities, culture and institutional relationships all play a role in the enabling of successful youth transitions. In providing an overview of this argument, this chapter goes on to highlight how and why this consideration must be woven into policy debates designed to improve the lives of the black community, not only in terms of youth and education matters, but also for wider social exclusion issues.

The chapter will now rehearse and discuss some of the themes and issues identified in the earlier chapters. We are interested both in the experiences and perspectives of young people and their significant others and in developing ways of understanding these experiences and perspectives theoretically.

Responding to Structural Inequality: The Place of 'Agency' and 'Success' as a Virtue

One of the pertinent points of contrast between the young people in our study and the representations of youth in contemporary policy and some sociological theorising rests upon the issue concerning the link between sections of the youth population leaving compulsory education with low or no educational qualifications and notions of 'agency', 'individualisation' and marginalisation (e.g. Beck, 1992; Furlong and Cartmel, 1997; Social Exclusion Unit, 1999a). It is suggested that the young people involved in this research would be identified as 'at risk' due to their societal position. This is due to the chances and opportunities that they are likely to receive or miss. Agency may play a part but invariably this is a 'bounded' (Evans et al, 2001) and 'limited, personal form of agency' (Wyn and White, 1998). Therefore it is necessary to understand the context and circumstances in which decisions and choices are made:

some of the problems faced by young people in modern Britain stem from an attempt to negotiate difficulties on an individual level. Blind to the existence of powerful chains of interdependency, young people frequently attempt to resolve collective problems through individual action and hold themselves responsible for their inevitable failure. (Furlong and Cartmel, 1997, p. 114)

We certainly do not want to deny that the structural position for young people can be overwhelming or that social structures have been weakened within risk society and late modernity to the extent that 'agency'/individualism is pre-eminent within social action. Yet we as 'empirical researchers seeking to make sense of the social' (Ball et al, 2000, p. 143) consider that central to the young people's biographies are themes interwoven with 'agency', family, community and social structures.

The biographical narratives of the young people concerning the difficulties encountered during the transitional phase, education and career paths explored in Chapters 2 and 4 highlight the ways in which black youth use their individual agency to survive and achieve within the educational system and post-compulsory schooling and in their subsequent careers, despite structural disadvantages. In relation to agency it seems that the young people operate within an 'opportunity structure bound' availed by their 'community orientation' which placed considerable emphasis on the individualistic motives of striving for success, but not the individualistic motives that Beck (1992) emphasises as most characteristic of the white middle classes. In this respect, agency is reflected through cultural practices, outlook and lifestyle. Our work indicated that agency is characterised first, despite their negative experiences of schooling, paradoxically the young people (and their families) held deep and abiding attachment to the value of education in terms of the scope for self-improvement and confidence building and a fierce determination to excel in educa-tion. In this respect, their disadvantaged schooling proved to be a motivating factor to succeed. Second, they utilised community-based networks, resources and significant others when confronted by problematic schooling situations and wider structural and societal constraints.

Our work certainly draws attention to the strategies that respondents employed in order to navigate success. The narratives from the respondents indicate that essential to their identity formation was the development of resilience, aspirations and ambitions that enabled them to achieve regardless of their negative educational experiences. For the majority of respondents re-engagement in education was considered essential to this. Indeed, Allen (1998) argues that black and ethnic minorities consider the acquisition of educational qualifications essential for instrumental and pragmatic reasons, such as economic and career success because of their perceived disadvantage in the labour market. These sentiments were echoed to a large extent amongst respondents who were united by the notion that education was a key to success. Moreover, the most dominant motivation for pursuing further and higher education was social mobility, expressed as wanting to 'make something of myself', 'get a proper job', 'prove them wrong'. The emphasis for most was clearly on the economic security benefits of a career, social status and the representation of blackness.

As signalled already, the arguments in this book have repositioned the main debates on exclusion, risk and youth transitions with particular reference to black youth. It has shown how agency, resistance and challenge are linked to the resources and opportunities that are made available through social and community capital (Bourdieu, 1986; Yosso, 2005). These resources are themselves facilitated through institutional relationships such as the family, kin and community-based organisations, and play a vital role in assisting successful transitions. This highlights the close interplay between 'agency' and 'structure'. This is the mobilisation of social resources, i.e. family, kin, community advocates and black cultural capital, in order to develop a positive sense of self, that then leads to the overcoming of exclusionary positions and reduces future chances of enhanced risk. However, this 'agency' and 'structure' connection is not a simple and linear one, not least because it works within a 'bounded' format (Evans, 2002). In other words, agency is bound by structured determinants, meaning that complex negotiations take place based on choices and constraints, which, of course, can in turn enhance or limit achievement (Skeggs, 1997).

Black Youth Transitions: The Role of Social Capital in Black Community Organisations

As mentioned above black youth carve out school-to-career transitions, overcome institutionalised racism, develop secure social relationships, and secure the social and community capital to construct oppositional representations and the confidence to defend a positive community identity. Crucially, these outcomes have occurred in relation to the structure of opportunities that prevail for them from the social/cultural/community capital made possible by families and community networks/organisations. This illustrates how alternative public spheres of community networks and family relationships encourage empowering narratives of identity, inclusion, social mobility and community. Through the prism of the community's response to structural educational inequality it is possible to extend the understanding of education, transitions and community service. Freire (1972) and hooks (1991) argue that education should achieve 'conscientisation', which is a social and political transformation. The relationship between education and an awareness of the politics of 'race' and the plight of youth was evident in the narratives of the respondents from the community provision highlighted in Chapter 5. Indeed, for some respondents political awareness and community activism informed their cultural practice. The majority felt that this was at the basis of understanding broader and longer-term processes of social reproduction and how exclusory transitions are made, or not. In this vein, the respondents expressed a desire to enhance the opportunities for future generations which suggests that their conscientisation (Freire, 1972) has taken place. Moreover, social bonding was also considered integral to the measures deployed in the community organisations' response to the adverse conditions experienced by black youth. As Ginwright (2007) argues:

> social capital consists of intergenerational ties that cultivate expectations about the capacity for Black youth to transform the conditions that shape their lives. For Black youth ... social capital is facilitated by challenging negative concepts about Black youth in public policy, developed by building racial solidarity, and sustained through political consciousness about personal issues. By examining how community

organizations cultivate a collective racial and political identity, we can develop a deep understanding of the intersection of social capital and collective action about Black youth [therefore] social capital moves beyond trust, connections to institutions, and relationships to illuminate the contours of how hope, faith, and optimism, serve as the ties that bind us together. (pp. 416–417)

Some Future Direction: Making Every Youth Matter

The arguments offered in this book are given with the intention that they be used to inform debates for policy formulation and best practice in matters regarding first, the educational services provided for black youth, and second, for other services designed to reduce the risk of exclusion and increase the status of black youth, i.e. health care, child and family support, housing, employment and criminal justice. In such areas the exclusionary impact has already been recognised by policy makers who have in recent years introduced a number of inclusion policies which have attempted to promote the idea of an inclusive and 'Learning Society' (Baron et al, 1999). In the UK, these changes have gained momentum since the New Labour Government set up the Social Exclusion Unit (Social Exclusion Unit, 1999a). They include the New Deal initiatives for 18–24-year-olds; Excellence in Cities; Education Action Zones; Further Education Colleges; Sure Start, The Learning Gateway and the Every Youth Matters agenda, which have also involved some changes being made in youth service provision. Similar attention to exclusion issues has also been given by the governments of other countries. However, one persistent problem remains and that is discrimination within these institutions. Despite attempts to promote best practice based on policies designed to fulfil the equality and diversity requirements of the inclusion agenda, as well as meeting requirements of relevant race equality legislation, it can be argued that a fair and desirable outcome has not truly emerged. This is largely as a result of persistent racially-based assumptions about problematic and troublesome black 'others', which is not least helped by increased market competition and privatisation. Indeed some suggest that inequalities have actually increased (Tomlinson, 2008).

In general, this policy domain tends to take a narrow approach to the adverse social and economic conditions faced by black youth. It has been demonstrated that one of the first areas where black youth directly encounters the barriers of a racist society is in education. Yet the misguided intervention of Widening Participation and similar agendas emphasises facilitating educational interest in black youth and works on 'discourses around "lifelong learning", the "learning society" and through concerns about "social exclusion", "disaffection" and "disillusionment with learning" ' (Archer and Yamashita, 2003, p. 53). In doing so, it fails to directly recognise and address the root problems of a discriminatory education system within a discriminatory society.

In addition, the value of the strategies for resistance and progression offered by the black community must be recognised, facilitated and supported. Here, some have presented an approach arguing that particular forms of social capital can be utilised as an 'alternative to social democratic welfare policies' (Field, 2003, p. 118). This has to some degree already been acknowledged. For example, it is certainly evident in the recent policies of the UK's New Labour Government, where there has been a reversal of the views about the value of supplementary schools and community-based mentoring programmes. However, these community-based organisations need to be more externally seriously acknowledged and financially supported, not least because they are in a position to offer an understanding of the cultural meanings attached by black people to matters of education, family, exclusion and capital (Rhamie, 2007). An indication of this is the recommendations given by the US-based group, the National Urban League (2009). In addressing directly the recently elected US President Barack Obama, the League's Report looks at the last five years' US Equality Index and notes how although progress in educational attainment for blacks was made, it was done so at a much slower rate than that of their white counterparts. As such, the League calls for continued work to reduce the discrimination and disadvantages faced by black people, not only in education, but also in wider social issues.

It is also argued here that those involved in policy and practice debates about youth service provisions, such as the Department for

Children and Families, the Equality and Human Rights Commission, and Local Education Authorities (LEAs) in the UK and those similar bodies in the US whose role it is to fulfil the 'Every Youth Matters' and 'No Child Left Behind' agendas, need to recognise that despite a nationally systemised school exclusion procedure having been in place for a number of years, the school exclusion rate for black young people remains disproportionately high. In light of this, there should be an active pursuit of a multi-pronged and multi-layered approach to an exclusion reduction programme (Rhamie, 2007). This should be done with radical targets, with the goal of reintegrating excludees into mainstream education. For this there should be a more financially accountable system in place which facilitates the movement of young people between institutions in their search to find a method of education appropriate to their requirements. The funding of schools should therefore return to a more centralised method. There should also be a consideration of alternative forms of assessment and measures of educational attainment. The National Urban League (2009) in particular calls for the replacement in the US of the Annual Yearly Progress report with a Comprehensive Accountability Framework that can 'more accurately capture student performance using multiple measures of achievement' (p. 9). This is seen as a more favourable option than recent education plans proposed by the UK government in their Raising Expectations Bill[1] (Department for Education and Skills, 2007), not least because the 'up skill' rationale fails to consider the existing problems that run throughout mainstream education. Bodies such as the Equality and Human Rights Commission and the National Urban League should give greater priority to assisting individual complainants from the black community and to initiating formal investigations into high excluding schools and authorities with demonstrable patterns of racial discrimination. In addition, LEAs and Local Authorities should work with schools to ensure that robust strategies are put in place to reduce school exclusion and to comply with the race equality legislation, such as the UK's Race Relations (Amendment) Act (2000), to ameliorate and tackle discrimination and disadvantage in this area. Additionally there needs to be an ongoing integrated support system in place to help excluded students to ensure their successful reintegration, as well as help avoid the risk of long-term exclusion in the wider society. It is important that all key contributors to this support system be given due recognition and funded accordingly in a more equal, authorised and appropriate way (National Urban League, 2009).

Concluding Comments

In conclusion, this book raises wider issues concerning the extent to which young people's transitions reflect continuing outcomes of structural inequality rather than personal agency or choice. For the young people in this study, adolescence was the time when they were at greater risk of experiencing exclusion from school. Difficulties experienced at school at the beginning of this period can then set the young person on a path which they may find impossible to change. This could be avoided by creating a different type of institution that caters for the needs of young people at that time when they are maturing into adults. In offering this analysis, it is hoped that a significant step forward can be made to cater for the needs of those who have been excluded from mainstream education as well as assisting successful transition into adulthood and avoiding further exclusion in wider society. To do this, changes, such as those outlined above, must be made. They must, though, be done in light of a recognition of the voices of those directly involved in cases of exclusion, such as the young people and their families. This would highlight the value of how agency, individual response, resistance, resilience and habitus all combine to allow black people to challenge and overcome the disadvantages that are thrown at them. To understand how and why this is done, their point of view must be listened to, respected and utilised to inform policy for progressive change. In doing so, lessons can be learnt not only for issues in education, but also for exclusion and social mobility matters in wider society regarding questions about the links between education, 'race', ethnicity, social justice and social stratification.

Notes

Introduction

1. Within the British education system the most serious sanction that a school can take against a student is to exclude them permanently. This is where a school decides to remove a student from the school role. The local education authority has a duty to ensure that such students receive a basic education elsewhere, often through placement in a special unit or limited separate tuition. However, permanent exclusion is only one form of school exclusion. Most school exclusion is of a fixed term with students readmitted after a period of time, usually one to five days. There is also a form of exclusion that occurs within the school: an internal exclusion where a student is removed from the classroom and placed in another room, an isolation room, to undertake school work.
2. Compulsory education in the UK covers the ages five to 16.
3. Standard Assessment Tests (SATs) refers to National Curriculum assessment of pupils at ages seven and 11.
4. At age 16 students in England and Wales normally take the GCSE (General Certificate of Secondary Education) examinations. This examination is the common form of high-stakes test currently taken by students at the end of their compulsory schooling. Compulsory schooling will shortly extend to 18 years. Separate subjects have their own GCSE examinations and good results are an essential part of the competition for places in further and higher education. GCSE results are graded A*, A, B, C, D, E, F and G, with U (ungraded) as a failing result. Although the other grades are officially counted as 'pass' grades, a common distinction is the greater status accorded the higher grade passes from A* to C inclusive.

5. The meaning of 'social exclusion' is unclear and open to interpretation. However, there is fairly common agreement on who constitute the socially excluded. These are usually taken to be those on low income, in poverty, had interrupted schooling, with a lack of qualifications and material disadvantage (Levitas, 1998). See also Chapter 1.

Chapter 1

1. The Labour Government launched the 'New Opportunities White Paper – Fair Chances for the Future', 13 January 2009 and the Equality Bill April 2009. Both the White Paper and the Bill are imbued with notions of 'social mobility'; the first sets out the Government's agenda for capturing the jobs of the future and investing in families, communities and citizens through their lives to help them get ahead, and the second aims to reduce inequalities (i.e. discrimination etc.) http:www.cabinetoffice.gov.uk/newsroom/news_release/2009/090113_newopportu ... http://www.commonsleader.gov.uk/output/page2657.asp
2. People who are graduates can expect many more years of higher paid employment than those who are not (for example Toynbee and Walker, 2008).
3. General National Vocational Qualification (GNVQ) and Business Technical Education Council (BTEC) qualifications are for age 16 to 19. They are vocational qualifications leading a student along a particular career route, for example Business, Health and Social Care, Engineering. Access courses are for students without the usual academic qualifications for university entry. They prepare students for a degree-level course.
4. Critical race theory (CRT) challenges how 'race' and racial power are constructed and represented in American legal culture and society. CRT has no specific doctrines or methodologies. Activism is part of CRT especially through community practice. CRT claims to be more systematic than anti-racism. Elements in CRT:

   • *Focus on racism:* Racism is regarded as normal and endemic and is what people of colour confront every day. Racism involves hidden and subtle operation of power that lead to ethnic minorities being disadvantaged; racism is not just acts of racism. Rather 'race' is socially constructed and changing.
   • *A critique of liberalism:* Claims of laws being neutral, objective, colour blind are camouflages that mark the interest of the power groups. Racial injustice is sustained behind the façade of laws to remedy racial inequality.
   • *A revisionist critique of civil rights law:* Traditional legal discourse only addresses crude versions of racism. Mainstream legal assumptions defend the status quo by being unable to address the ingrained racism. Meritocracy is a myth.

- *Importance of experiential knowledge:* Report viewpoints and experiences of minorities groups.

Conceptual/methodological tools relating to CRT include:

1 *Storytelling:* A construction of narratives out of live realities.
2 *Interest convergence:* Racial advances are tolerated for blacks only if they promote white self-interest, e.g. the main beneficiaries of affirmative action have been white women.
3 *Increasing focus on white studies and whiteness:* All white people are seen as benefiting from racism although differentially. All white people are implicated in white supremacy.
4 *White supremacy:* This is the operation of forces that shape the interests of white people. It is the subordination of people of colour to white privilege.

Chapter 2

1. This is largely due to the changes in the UK labour market which now make it difficult for post-16-year-olds to obtain a job.

Chapter 4

1. Subcultural theory emerged out of the 1960s and 1970s with the combining of many underlying factors with definitions of youth and delinquency. This theory looked at anti-school culture, adopted by boys, where subcultures or 'subcultures of resistance' fulfilled the leisure time of young people due to the 'meaninglessness' of school. The notion of subcultures of resistance was developed from the influential work of cultural reproductionists who in the late 1970s dominated the analysis of social inequality in Britain. This theory suggests that through their own activity and ideological development, young working-class men and women reproduce themselves as working class.
2. Criticism of this study, together with the theory in forming it, ranges from over-romanticising working-class youth cultures to their detriment (Brown, 1987) to creating a distinct dualism between working-class culture and middle-class culture, ignoring the resistance of young women (McRobbie and Garber, 1976).
3. Very little work exists on the experiences of young black women, other than that conducted in the area of education: an exception is Weekes, 'Shades of blackness: young women contradictions of beauty', in Mirza, 1997.

Chapter 6

1. US First Lady Michelle Obama's speech at London's Elisabeth Garrett Anderson school, during her visit to the UK, April 2009. It was a speech made to a girls-only inner-city school, 92% of the students of which are from a black or minority background (*Observer*, 5 April 2009, pp. 22–23).
2. A consistent finding in both the USA and UK is that where education systems use some form of internal differentiation through tracking, setting, banding, streaming, black students are usually overrepresented in the lowest status groups (e.g. Wright, 1987; Banks and Banks, 2000; Gillborn and Mirza, 2000).
3. As second generation parents of Caribbean background are likely to show a strong commitment to education and would also identify with the meritocratic ideal of 'getting on' through education (e.g. see Foner, 1979).

Chapter 7

1. On a data set that showed that post-16 education participation rates were very low in the UK, this Bill proposed that all people in England should participate in education or training until their 18th birthday (Department for Education and Skills, 2007). The rationale was based on the view that to 'up skill' a workforce in this way would give the country stronger economic success in terms of its global status, as well as improve the social well-being of citizens (Simmons, 2008, p. 420).

References

Ahier, J., & Moore, R. (1999). Post-16 education, semi-independent youth and the privatisation of inter-age transfers: Re-theorising youth transition. *British Journal of Sociology of Education, 20,* (4), 515–530.

Ahmed, S. (2005). What is the evidence of early intervention, preventative services for black and minority ethnic group children and their families? *Practice, 17,* (2), 89–101.

Akom, A. A. (2003). Reexamining resistance as oppositional behaviour: The Nation of Islam and the creation of a Black achievement ideology. *Sociology of Education, 76,* (4), 305–325.

Aldridge, S. (2003). The facts about social mobility: A survey of recent evidence on social mobility and its cause. *New Economy, 10,* (4), 189–193.

Alexander, C. E. (1996). *The art of being black: The creation of black British youth identities.* Oxford: Oxford University Press.

Alexander, C. E. (2000). *The Asian gang.* Oxford/New York: Berg.

Alex-Assensoh, Y. M. (2004). Taking the sanctuary to the streets: Religion, race and community development in Columbus, Ohio. *Annals of the American Academy of Political and Social Science, 7,* 79–91.

Allen, D. (2002). Research involving vulnerable young people: A discussion of ethical and methodological concerns. *Drugs: Education, Prevention and Policy, 9,* (3), 275–283.

Allen, S. (1998). What are ethnic minorities looking for? In T. Modood, & T. Acland (Eds.), *Race and higher education experiences, challenges and policy implications* (pp. 51–73). London: Policy Studies Institute, University of Westminster.

Alleyne, B. (2002). *Radicals against race.* Oxford: Berg.

Alperson, P. (2002). *Diversity and community: An interdisciplinary reader.* Oxford: Blackwell Publishers Limited.

Anderson, B. (1983). *Imagined communities*. London: Verso.

Anderson, E. (1990). *Streetwise: Race, class, and change in an urban community*. Chicago: University of Chicago Press.

Anderson, E. (1999). *Code of the streets: Decency, violence, and the moral life of the inner city*. New York: Norton.

Anthias, F., & Yuval-Davis, N. (1992) *Racialised boundaries: Race, nation, gender, colour and class and the anti-racist struggle*. London: Routledge.

Anyon, J. (1997). *Ghetto schooling: A political economy of urban education reform*. New York: Teacher College.

Appiah, L. (2001). *Mentoring: School-business links*. London: Runnymede Trust.

Apple, M. (2004). Between neo and post: Critique and transformation in critical educational studies. In G. Ladson-Billings, & D. Gillborn (Eds.), *The RoutledgeFalmer reader in multicultural education* (pp. 211–244). London: RoutledgeFalmer.

Archer, L., & Francis, B. (2007). *Understanding minority ethnic achievement: Race, gender, class and 'success'*. London and New York: Routledge.

Archer, L., & Yamashita, H. (2003). 'Knowing their limits'? Identities, inequalities and inner city school leavers' post-16 aspirations. *Journal of Education Policy, 18*, (1), 53–69.

Attwood, G., Croll, P., & Hamilton, J. (2004). 'Re-engaging with education', *Research Papers in Education, 2*, (1), 75–95.

Ball, S. (2003). *Class strategies and the education market*. London: RoutledgeFalmer.

Ball, S., Maguire, M., & Macrae, S. (2000). *Choice, pathways and transitions post 16: New youth, new economies in the global city*. London: RoutledgeFalmer.

Banks, J. A., & Banks, C. A. (1995–2001). *Handbook of research on multicultural education*. (2nd ed.) San Francisco, CA: Jossey-Bass.

Barn, R. (2001). *Black youth on the margins: A research review*. York: Joseph Rowntree Foundation.

Baron, S., Riddell, S., & Wilson, A. (1999). The secret of eternal youth: Identity, risk and learning difficulties. *British Journal of Sociology of Education, 20*, (4), 483–499.

Bay Area School Reform Collaborative (BASRC) (2003). *Research Brief, January 2001*. USA: BASRC.

Beck, U. (1992). *Risk society: Towards a new modernity*. London: Sage.

Becker, H. S. (1952). Social class variations in pupil-teacher relationships. *Journal of Educational Sociology, 25*, 451–465.

Bell, D. (1995). Who's afraid of critical race theory? *University of Illinois Law Review 1995*, 892–910.

Bhattacharyya, G., Ison, I., & Blair, M. (2003). *Minority ethnic attainment and participation in education and training: The evidence*. London: DFES.

Bhavnani, K., & Pheonix, A. (1994). *Shifting identities, shifting racism: A feminism and psychology reader*. London: Sage.

Bhui, K. (2002). *Racism and mental health: Prejudice and suffering*. London: Jessica Kinsgsley.

Blair, M. (2001). *Why pick on me?* Stoke-on-Trent: Trentham Books.

Blanden, J., Goodman, A., Gregg, P., & Machin, S. (2002). Changes in intergenerational mobility in Britain. *Centre for the Economics of Education, Discussion Paper No: CEEDP0026.*

Blanden, J., Goodman, A., Gregg, P., & Machin, S. (2004). Changes in intergenerational mobility in Britain. In M. Corak (Ed.), *Generational income mobility in North America and Europe* (pp. 147–158). Cambridge: Cambridge University Press.

Blanden, J., Gregg, P., & Machin, S. (2005). *Intergenerational mobility in Europe and North America.* London: London School of Economics, Centre for Economic Performance.

Blumer, H. (1969). *Symbolic interactionism: Perspective and method.* New Jersey: Prentice Hall.

Bourdieu, P. (1986). The forms of capital. In J. E. Richardson (Ed.), *Handbook of theory of research for sociology of education* (pp. 241–258). New York: Greenwood Press.

Bourdieu, P., & Passeron, J.-C. (1977). *Reproduction in education, society and culture.* London: Sage.

Bourne, J., Bridges, L., & Searle, C. (1994). *Outcast England: How schools exclude black children.* London: Institute of Race Relations.

Bowling, B., & Philips, C. (2002). *Racism, crime and justice.* Longman: London.

Brah, A. (1996). *Cartographies of diaspora: Contesting identities.* London: Routledge.

Brah, A., & Minhas, R. (1986). Structural racism or cultural differences: Schooling for Asian girls. In G. Weiner (Ed.), *Just a bunch of girls* (pp. 128–147). Milton Keynes: Open University Press.

Brah, A., & Phoenix, A. (2004). Ain't I a woman?: Revisiting intersectionality. *Journal of International Women's Studies, 5,* (3), 75–86.

Branglinger, E. (2003). *Dividing classes: How the middle class negotiates and rationalises school advantage.* New York: Routledge.

Brown, P. (1987). *Schooling ordinary boys.* London: Tavistock.

Bynner, J. (2001). British youth transitions in comparative perspective. *Journal of Youth Studies, 4,* 5–23.

Callender, C., & Wright, C. (2001). Discipline and democracy: Race, gender, school sanctions and control. In M. Arnot, & J. Dillabough (Eds.), *Gender, education and citizenship: An international feminist reader* (pp. 216–237). London: Routledge.

Carby, H. (1982). White woman listen! Black feminism and the boundaries of sisterhood. In P. Gilroy (Ed.), *The empire strikes back: Race and racism in 70s Britain* (pp. 212–235). London: Hutchinson.

Carter, D. J. (2005). In a sea of white people: An analysis of the experiences and behaviours of high achieving black students in a predominantly white school. Doctoral dissertation: Harvard Graduate School of Education.

Casey, K. (1993). *I answer with my life: Life histories of women teachers working for social change.* New York: Routledge.

Cashmore, E. E. (1979). *Rastaman: The Rastafarian movement in England.* London: Allen & Unwin.

Channer, Y. (1995). *I am a promise: The school achievement of British African-Caribbeans*. Stoke on Trent: Trentham Books.

Cheetham, J. (1986). Introduction. In S. Ahmed, J. Cheetham, & J. Small (Eds.), *Social work with black children and their families*. London: Batsford/BAAF.

Christian, M. (1998). 'Empowerment and black communities in the UK, with special reference to Liverpool'. *Community Development Journal, 33*, (1), 18–31.

Christian, M. (2005). The politics of black presence in Britain and black male exclusion in the British education system. *Journal of Black Studies, 35*, (3), 327–281.

Cieslik, M. (2001). Researching youth cultures: Some problems with the cultural turn in British youth studies. *Scottish Youth Issues Journal, 1*, (2), 27–47.

Coard, B. (1971). *How the West Indian child is made educationally subnormal in the British school system*. London: New Beacon Books.

Cohen, P. (1997). *Re-thinking the youth question: Education, labour and cultural studies*. Hampshire: Macmillian Press Limited.

Cohen, P., & Ainley, P. (2000). In the country of the blind? Youth studies and cultural studies in Britain. *Journal of Youth Studies, 3*, (1), 79–95.

Cohen, S. (1980). *Folk devils and moral panics*. Oxford: Martin Robertson.

Cohen, R., & Hughes, M. with Ashworth, L., & Blair, M. (1994). *School's out: The family perspective on school exclusion*. Essex: Family Service Unit.

Colley, H., & Hodkinson, P. (2001). Problems with bridging the gap: The reversal of structure and agency in addressing social exclusion. *Critical Social Policy, 21*, (3), 335–359.

Collins, P. H. (1990). *Black feminist thought: Knowledge, consciousness and the politics of empowerment*. London: Routledge.

Cork, L. (2005). *Supporting black pupils and parents: Understanding and improving home–school relations*. London: Routledge.

Craig, G. (2000). *Reaching disaffected youth*. Lincoln: Lincolnshire TEC.

Cregan, C. (2002). Are things really getting better? The labour market experience of black and female youth at the start of the century. *Capital and Class, 77*, Summer, 23–52.

Crenshaw, K. W. (1991). Mapping the margins: Intersectionality, identity politics, and violence against women of colour. *Stanford Law Review, 43*, (6), 1241–1299.

Crenshaw, K., Gotanda, N., Peller, G., & Thomas, K. (1995). *Critical race theory: The key writings that formed the movement*. New York: New Press.

Crozier, G. (2001). Excluded parents: The deracialisation of parental involvement. *Race, Ethnicity and Education, 12*, (4), 329–341.

Dean, H. (1997). Underclassed or undermined? Young people and social citizenship. In R. MacDonald (Ed.), *Youth, the 'underclass' and social exclusion* (pp. 55–69). London: Routledge.

Dean, H. (2003). Re-conceptualising Welfare-To-Work for people with multiple problems and needs. *Journal of Social Policy, 32*, (3), 441–459.

Department for Education and Employment (1999). *Learning to succeed: A new framework for post-16 learning.* London: The Stationery Office.

Department for Education and Employment (2000a). *Connexions: Connexions service prospectus and specification.* London: HMSO.

Department for Education and Employment (2000b). *Statistics of Education, Permanent Exclusions from maintained schools in England (10/00).* London: DfES.

Department of Education and Science (DES) (1985). *Education for All* (The Swann Report). London: HMSO.

Department for Education and Skills (2003). *Statistics of education, permanent exclusions from schools and exclusion appeals: England 2001/2002 (provisional)* (SFR 16/2003). London: DfES.

Department for Education and Skills (2006). *Ethnicity and education: The evidence on minority ethnic pupils aged 5–16.* Nottingham: DfES.

Department for Education and Skills (2007). *Raising expectations: Staying in education and training post-16.* Norwich: The Stationery Office.

Dewan, I. (2005). An investigation into personhood and equity, with special reference to mixed-race women in post-compulsory education. Unpublished PhD thesis, London: University of Greenwich.

Dove, N. (1998). *Afrikan mothers: Bearers of culture, makers of social change.* New York: Albany.

Du Bois-Reymond, M. (1998). 'I don't want to commit myself yet': Young people's life concepts. *Journal of Youth Studies, 1,* (1), 63–79.

Duneier, M. (1992). *Slim's table: Race, respectability and masculinity.* Chicago: University of Chicago Press.

Edmunds, A. (2000). *Youth work and youth crime: Guide to policy and practice.* Place Youth Work Press.

Education Trust (2006). *Funding gaps 2006.* Washington, DC: The Education Trust.

Eggleston, J., Dunn, D., Anjali, M., & Wright, C. (1986). *Education for some.* Stoke-on-Trent: Trentham Books.

Eitle, D. (2004). Inequality, segregation, and the overrepresentation of African Americans in school suspensions. *Sociological Perspectives, 47,* (3), 269–287.

Evans, K. (2002). Taking control of their lives? Agency in youth adult transitions in England and New Germany. *Journal of Youth Studies, 5,* (3), 245–269.

Evans, K., Rudd, P., Behren, M., Kaluze, J., & Woolley, C. (2001). Reconstructing fate as choice? *Youth, 9,* (3), 2–28.

Field, J. (2003). *Social capital.* London: Routledge.

Foner, N. (1979). *Jamaica farewell: Jamaican migration in London.* London: RKP.

Fordham, S. (1996). *Blacked out: Dilemmas of race, identity, and success at Capital High.* Chicago, IL: University of Chicago Press.

Fraser, N. (1994). Rethinking the public sphere: A continuation to the critique of actually existing democracy. In H. A. Giroux, & P. Mclean (Eds.), *Between borders: Pedagogy and the politics of cultural studies.* New York: Routledge.

Freire, P. (1972). *Pedogogy of the oppressed.* London: Penguin Books.

Frost, S., Phoenix, A., & Pattman, R. (2002). *Young masculinities.* New York: Palgrave Ltd.

Fuller, M. (1982). Young, female and black. In E. Cashmore, & B. Troyna (Eds.), *Black youth in crisis* (pp. 87–99). London: George Allen & Unwin.

Fuller, M. (1984). Black girls in a London comprehensive school. In M. Hammersley, & P. Woods (Eds.), *Life in schools: The sociology of pupil culture.* Milton Keynes: Open University Press.

Furlong, A., & Cartmel, E. (1997). *Young people and social change: Individualization and risk in late modernity.* Milton Keynes: OUP.

Gardner, R., Ford, D.Y., & Miranda, A. H. (2001). Education of African American students: The struggle continues. *The Journal of Negro Education,* Fall, 212–224.

Genero, N. P. (1998). Culture, resiliency and mutual psychological development. In H. I. McCubbin, E. A. Thompson, A. I. Thompson, & J. A. Futrell (Eds.), *Resiliency in African-American families* (pp. 31–48). London: Sage.

Gibson, M. A. (1988). *Accommodation without assimilation: Sikh immigration in an American high school.* Ithaca, NY: Cornell University Press.

Giddens, A. (1991). *Modernity and self identity: Self and society in late modernity.* Cambridge: Polity.

Gillborn, D. (1990). *Race, ethnicity and education: Teaching and learning in multi-ethnic schools.* London: Unwin Hyman.

Gillborn, D. (1998). Racism and the politics of qualitative research: Learning from controversy and critique. In P. Connolly, & B. Troyna (Eds.), *Researching racism in education: Politics, theory and practice* (pp. 34–54). Buckinghamshire: Open University Press.

Gillborn, D. (2005). Education policy as an act of white supremacy: Whiteness, critical race theory and education reform. *Journal of Education Policy, 20,* (4), 485–505.

Gillborn, D. (2008). *Racism and education: Coincidence or conspiracy?* London: Routledge.

Gillborn, D., & Gipps, C. (1996). *Recent research on the achievement of ethnic minority pupils.* London: The Stationery Office.

Gillborn, D., & Mirza, H. (2000). *Mapping class, gender and race.* London: OFSTED.

Gilroy, P. (1987). *There ain't no black in the union jack.* Chicago, IL: Chicago University Press.

Ginwright, S. A. (2007). Black youth activism and the role of critical social capital in black community organizations. *American Behavioural Scientist, 51,* (3), 403–418.

Goffman, E. (1963). *Stigma: Notes on the management of a spoiled identity.* London: Penguin.

Goldthorpe, J. H. (1996). Class analysis and the re-orientation of class theory: The case of persisting differentials in education attainment. *British Journal of Sociology, 45,* (3), 481–505.

Goldthorpe, J. (2004). Trends in intergenerational mobility in Britain in the late twentieth century. In R. Breen (Ed.), *Social mobility in Europe* (pp. 195–225). Oxford: Oxford University Press.

Goulbourne, H. (1999). The transnational character of Caribbean kinship in Britain. In S. McRae (Ed.), *Changing Britain: Families and households in the 1990s* (pp. 176–197). Oxford: Oxford University Press.

Goulbourne, H. (2002). *Caribbean transnational experience.* London: Pluto Press.

Goulbourne, H., & Solomos, J. (2003). Families, ethnicity and social capital. *Social Policy and Society 2*, (4), 329–338.

Graham, J., & Bowling, B. (1995). *Young people and crime* (HO Research Study No. 145). London: The Stationery Office.

Graham, M. (2002). Creating spaces: Exploring the role of cultural knowledge as a source of empowerment in models of social welfare in black communities. *British Journal of Social Work, 32*, (1), 35–49.

Graham, M. (2004). Empowerment revisited: Social work, resistance and agency in black communities. *European Journal of Social Work, 7*, (1), 43–56.

Gramsci, A. (1971). *Selections from prison notebooks.* London: Lawrence and Wishart Ltd.

Granovetter, M. (1973). The strength of weak ties. *American Journal of Sociology*, 78, 1360–1380.

Green, A., Maguire, M., & Canny, A. (2001). *Keeping track: Mapping and tracking vulnerable young people.* Bristol: Policy Press.

Green, E., Mitchell, W., & Bunton, R. (2000). Contextualising risk and danger: An analysis of young people's perceptions of risk. *Journal of Youth Studies, 3*, (2), 109–126.

Griffiths, M. (1998). *Education research for social justice: Getting off the fence.* Buckingham: Open University Press

Guardian (10 November 2008). URL: http://www.guardian.co.uk/politics/blog/2008/nov/10/barackobama-race

Hall, S. (1996). Who needs identity? In S. Hall, & P. du Gay (Eds.), *Questions of cultural identity* (pp. 1–17). London: Sage.

Harris, N., & Eden, K., with Blair, A. (2000). *Challenges to school exclusion: Exclusion, appeals, the law.* London: Routledge.

Hayden, C. A. (1996). *Explaining exclusion from primary school: An analysis of the reasons behind the rise in recorded primary school exclusions in the early 1990s.* Ph.D. thesis, University of Portsmouth.

Hayden, C. A., & Dunne, S. (2001). *Outside looking in: Children and families' experience of social exclusion.* London: The Children's Society.

Heath, A., & McMahon, D. (2005). Social mobility of ethnic minorities. In G. Loury, T. Modood, & S. Teles (Eds.), *Ethnicity, social mobility and public policy* (pp. 393–413). Cambridge: Cambridge University Press.

Hernstein, R., & Murray, C. (1994). *The bell curve: Intelligence and class structure in American life.* New York: Free Press.

Hill, R. (1971). *The strength of black families.* New York: Emerson-Hall.

Hills, J., Le Grand, J., & Piachaud, D. (Eds.) (2002). *Understanding social exclusion.* Oxford: Oxford University Press.

hooks, b. (1989). *Talking back: Thinking feminism, thinking black.* London: Sheba Feminist.

hooks, b. (1991). *Yearning: Race, gender and cultural politics.* Boston, MA: Turnaround.

Hylton, C. (1996). *Family survival strategies: Ways of coping in UK society.* London: Exploring Parenthood.

Institute of Race Relations (1981). *Southall: The birth of a black community.* London: IRR and Southall Rights.

Jeffrey, C., & McDowell, L. (2004). Youth in a comparative perspective: Global change, local lives. *Youth and Society, 36,* (2), 131–142.

Jenkins, R. (1996). *Social identity.* London: Routledge.

Jones, A., Jeyasingham, D., & Rajasooriya, S. (2002). *Invisible families: The strengths and needs of black families in which young people have caring responsibilities.* York: Joseph Rowntree Foundation.

Jones, G. (2002). *The youth divide.* York: Joseph Rowntree Foundation/York Publishing Services.

Jones, L. (1984). White-black achievement differences. *American Sociological Review, 39,* (11), 1207–1213.

King, J. (Ed.) (2005). *Black education: A transformative research and action agenda for the new century.* New Jersey: Lawrence Erlbaum Associates.

Klein, R. (1995). Escape route from the fire of alienation: Status of black students in British schools. *Times Educational Supplement,* 10 February 1995, 10.

Ladson-Billings, G. (2006). From the achievement gap to the education debt: Understanding achievement in U.S schools. *Educational Researcher, 35,* (7), 3–12.

Ladson-Billings, G., & Tate, W. F. (1995). Toward a critical theory of education. *Teacher College Record, 97,* 47–68.

Lambert, L., & Streather, J. (1980). *Children in changing families: A study of adoption and illegitimacy.* London: Macmillan.

Levitas, R. (1998). *The inclusive society?* Basingstoke: Macmillan.

Liu, G. (2006). Inter-state inequality in educational opportunity. *New York University Law Review, 81,* (6), 2044–2156.

Logan, S. L. (1996). Strengthening family ties: Working with black female single-parent families. In S. L. Logan (Ed.), *The black family: Strengths, self-help and positive change.* Kansas: Westview Press.

Loury, C., Modood, T., & Teles, S. (2005). *Ethicity, social mobility and public policy.* Cambridge: Cambridge University Press.

Mac an Ghaill, M. (1988). *Young, gifted and black: Student–teacher relations in the schooling of black youth.* Buckingham: Open University Press.

Mac an Ghaill, M. (1994). *The making of men.* Buckingham: Open University Press.

MacDonald, R. (Ed.) (1997). *Youth, the 'underclass' and social exclusion.* London: Routledge.

MacDonald, R., & Marsh, J. (2001). Disconnected youth. *Journal of Youth Studies*, *4*, (4), pp. 373–391.

MacDonald, R. J., & Marsh, J. (2004). Missing school: Educational engagement, youth transitions and social exclusion. *Youth and Society*, *36*, (2), 143–162.

MacDonald, R., & Marsh, J. (2005). *Disconnected youth? Growing up in Britain's poor neighbourhoods*. Basingstoke: Palgrave.

MacDonald, R., Mason, P., Shildrick, T., Webster, C., Johnson, L., & Ridley, L. (2001). Snakes and ladders: In defence of studies of transition. *Sociological Research Online*, *5*, (4). URL: http://www.socesonline.org.uk/5/4/macdonald.

MacDonald, R., Shildrick, T., Webster, C., & Simpson, D. (2005). Growing up in poor neighbourhoods: The significance of class and place in the extended transitions of 'socially excluded' young adults. *Sociology*, *39*, (5), 873–891.

Macpherson, W. (1999). *The Stephen Lawrence enquiry: Report by Sir William Macpherson*. London: The Stationery Office.

Macrae, S., Maguire, M., & Milbourne, L. (2003). Social exclusion: Exclusion from school. *International Journal of Inclusive Education*, *7* (2), 89–101.

Majors, R. (Ed.) (2001). *Educating our black children*. London: Routledge.

Manns, W. (1996). Supportive role of significant others in black families. In H. P. McAdoo (Ed.), *Black families* (pp. 270–283). London: Sage.

May, C., & Cooper, A. (1995). Personal identity and social change: Some theoretical considerations. *Acta Sociologica*, *38*, (1), 75–85.

McAdoo, H. P. (Ed.) (1998). *Black families*. London: Sage.

McLeod, J., & Yates, L. (2006). *Making modern lives: Subjectivity, schooling and social change*. New York: SUNY.

McRobbie, A. (1990). *Feminism and youth culture*. London: Macmillan.

McRobbie, A., & Garber, J. (1976). Girls and subcultures: An exploration. In S. Hall, & T. Jefferson (Eds.), *Resistance through rituals: Youth subculture in post war Britain* (pp. 53–70). London: Hutchinson.

Mead, G. H. (1995). Self. In F. Anthias, & M. P. Kelly (Eds.), *Sociological debates: Thinking about the social* (pp. 361–364). Kent: Greenwich University Press.

Merton, M. (1998). *Finding the missing*. Leicester: Youth Work Press.

Miles, S. (1998). *Consumerism – as a way of life*. London: Sage.

Miles, S. (2000). *Youth lifestyles in a changing world*. Buckingham: Open University Press.

Milne, A., Myers, D., Rosenthal, A., & Ginsburg, A. (1986). Single parents, working mothers and the educational achievement of school children. *Sociology of Education*, *59*, 125–139.

Mirza, H. S. (1992). *Young, female and black*. London: Routledge.

Mirza, H. S. (1997). Black women in education: A collective movement for social change. In H. S. Mirza (Ed.), *Black British feminism* (pp. 269–277). London: Routledge.

Mirza, H. (2004). Black women in education: A collective movement for social change. In G. Ladson-Billings, & D. Gillborn (Eds.), *Multicultural education: The Routledge Falmer reader* (pp. 201–208). London: Routledge Falmer.

Mirza, H. S., & Reay, D. (2000). Spaces and places of black educational desire: Rethinking black supplementary schools as a new social movement. *Sociology, 34*, (3), 521–544.

Mitchell, W., Crawshaw, P., Burton, R., & Green. E. E. (2001). Situating young people's experiences of risk and identity. *Health, Risk and Society, 3*, (2), 217–233.

Modood, T. (2005). Ethnicity and political mobilization in Britain. In G. Loury, T. Modood, & S. Teles (Eds.), *Ethnicity, social mobility and public policy* (pp. 457–474). Cambridge: Cambridge University Press.

Modood, T., Berthoud, R., Lakey, J., Nazroo, J., Smith, P., Verdee, S., & Beishon, S. (1997). *Ethnic minorities in Britain, diversity and disadvantage*. London: Policy Studies Institute.

Mullard, C. (1985). Multiracial education in Britain. In M. Arnot (Ed.), *Race and gender: Equal opportunities policies in education*. Milton Keynes: Open University Press.

National Urban League (2009). *The state of black America 2009: Message to the President: Executive summary*. New York: NUL.

Natriello, G., & McDill, E. L. (1986). Performance standards, student effort on homework and academic achievement. *Sociology of Education, 59*, 18–31.

Nembhard, J. G., & Pang, V. O. (2003). Ethnic youth programs: Teaching about caring economic communities and self-empowered leadership. In G. Ladson-Billings (Ed.), *Critical race theory perspectives on social studies: The profession, policies and curriculum* (pp. 98–120). Connecticut: Information Age Publishing.

Norguera, P. (1995). Preventing and producing violence: A critical analysis of responses to school violence. *Harvard Educational Review, 65*, (2), 189–212.

Nowotny, H. (1981). Women in public life in Australia. In C. Fuchs, D. Epstein, & R. Coser (Eds.), *Access to power: Cross-national studies of women and elites*. London: George Allen & Unwin.

Nunn, A. Johnson, S., Moun, S., Bricherstaffe, T., & Kelsey, S. (2007). *Factors influencing social mobility: A report of research carried out by the Policy Research Institute on behalf of the Department for Work and Pensions Corporate Document Services* (Research Report No. 450). London: DWP.

Nussbaum, M. (2004). *Hiding from humanity: Disgust, shame and the law*. Princeton, NJ: Princeton University Press.

O'Donnell, M., & Sharpe, S. (2004). The social construction of youthful masculinities: peer group sub-cultures. In S. Ball (Ed.), *The Routledge Falmer reader in sociology of education* (pp. 89–127). London: Routledge Falmer.

OFSTED (1996). *Exclusion from secondary schools, 1995–6: A report from HMCI*. London: The Stationery Office.

OFSTED (2001). *Improving attendance and behaviour in secondary schools*. London: OFSTED.

Ogbu, J. (1974). *The next generation: An ethnography of education in an urban neighbourhood.* New York: Academic Press.

Ogbu, J. (1978). *Minority education and caste: The American system in cross-cultural perspectives.* New York: Academic Press.

Orr, A. J. (2003). Black-white differences in achievement: The importance of wealth. *Sociology of Education, 76,* (4), 281–304.

Osler, A., Street, C., Lall, M., & Vincent, C. (2002). *Girls and school exclusion.* York: Joseph Rowntree Foundation.

Ovenden, C., & Loxley, W. (1993). Getting teenagers to talk: Methodological considerations in planning and implementation of the youth Aids and drugs study. *Health Promotional Journal of Australia, 3,* 26–30.

Owen, D. (1977). A demographic profile of Caribbean households and families in Great Britain. In Centre for Ethnic Relations Living Arrangements, Family Structure and Social Change of Caribbean in Britain: ERSC populations and household change research programme, Coventry of Warwick.

Page, D. (2000). *Communities in the balance: The reality of social exclusion on housing estates.* York: Joseph Rowntree Foundation.

Parekh, B. (2000). *The future of multi-ethnic Britain.* London: Profile Books Ltd.

Parsons, C. (1999). *Education, exclusion and citizenship.* London: Routledge.

Parsons, C., & Castle, F. (1999). The economics of exclusion. In C. Parsons (Ed.), *Education, exclusion and citizenship* (pp. 89–106). London: Routledge.

Parsons, C., Castle, F., Hawlett, K., & Worrall, J. (1996). *Exclusion from school: The public cost.* London: Commission for Racial Equality.

Parsons, C., Godfrey, R., Annan, G., Cornwall, J., Dussart, M., Hepburn, S., Howlett, K., & Wennerstrom, V. (2004). *Minority ethnic exclusions and the Race Relations (Amendment) Act 2000* (Research Report 616). London: Department for Education and Skills.

Patel, T. G. (2008). *Mixed up kids? Race, identity and social order.* Dorset: Russell House Publishers.

Perri 6 (1997). *Escaping poverty: From safety nets to networks of opportunity.* London: Demos.

Perry, T. (2003). Up from the parched earth. In T. Perry, C. Steel, & A. Hillard III (Eds.), *Young gifted and black: Promoting high achievement among African-American students* (pp. 1–10). Boston: Beacon.

Phoenix, A. (2001). Positioned by 'hegemonic' masculinities: A study of London boys' narratives of identity. *Australian Psychologist, 36,* (1), 27–35.

Pomeroy, E. (2000). *Experiencing exclusion.* Stoke on Trent: Trentham Books.

Prevatt Goldstein, B., & Spencer, M. (2000). *Race and ethnicity: A consideration of issues for black, minority ehnic and white children in family placement.* London: BAAF.

Prince's Trust, The (2002). *The way it is: Young people on race, school exclusion and leaving care.* London: The Prince's Trust.

Prins, B. (2006). Narrative accounts of origins: A blind spot in the intersectionality. *European Journal of Women's Studies, 13,* (3), 188–192.

Pryce, K. (1967). *Endless pressure.* Harmondsworth: Penguin.

Putnam, R. D. (1995). Bowling alone: America's declining social capital. *Journal of Democracy, 6,* (1), 65–78.

Race Relations (Amendment) Act (2000). London: The Stationery Office.

Raffo, C. (2003). Disaffected young people and the work-related curriculum at Key Stage 4: Issues of social capital development and learning as a form of cultural practice. *Journal of Education and Work, 16,* (1), 70–86.

Rashid, S. P. (2000). The strengths of black families: Appropriate placements for all. *Adoption and Fostering, 24,* (1), 15–21.

Ratcliffe, P. (2004). *'Race', ethnicity and difference.* London: Open University Press.

Reay, D. (2000). A useful extension of Bourdieu's conceptual framework? Emotional capital as a way of understanding mothers' involvement in their children's education? *Sociological Review, 48,* (44), 568–585.

Reay, D., & Mirza, H. (1997). Uncovering genealogies of the margins: Black supplement Schooling. *British Journal of Sociology of Education, 18,* (4), 477–499.

Reynolds, T. (2004). *Caribbean families, social capital and young people's diasporic identities.* London: South Bank University.

Reynolds, T. (2005). *Caribbean mothers: Identity and experience in the UK.* London: The Tufnell Press.

Reynolds, T. (2006). Caribbean families, social capital and young people's diasporic identities. *Ethnic and Racial Studies, 2,* (6), 1087–1103.

Reynolds, T. (2008). *Ties that bind: Families, social capital and Caribbean second-generation return migration.* London: South Bank University.

Rhamie, J. (2007). *Eagles who soar: How black learners find the path to success.* Stoke on Trent: Trentham Books.

Rhamie, J., & Hallam, S. (2002). An investigation into African-Caribbean academic success. *Race, Ethnicity and Education, 5,* (2), 151–170.

Roza, M., & Hill, P. (2004). How within-distinct spending inequalities help some schools fail. In D. Ravitch (Ed.), *Brookings papers on education policy: 2004* (pp. 201–227). Washington, DC: Brookings Institution.

Rudd, P., & Evans, K. (1998). Structure and agency in youth transitions: Students' experience of vocational education. *Journal of Youth Studies, 1,* (1), 39–63.

Sampson, R. J., Morenoff, J. D., & Earls, F. (1999). Beyond social capital: Spatial dynamics of collective efficacy for children. *American Sociological Review, 64,* 633–660.

Sewell, T. (1997). *Black masculinities and schooling: How black boys survive modern schooling.* Stoke on Trent: Trentham Books.

Sewell, W. (1992). A theory of structure: Duality, agency and transformation. *American Journal of Sociology, 98,* (1), 1–29.

Shiner, M., & Modood, T. (2002). Help or hindrance? Higher education and the route to ethnic equality. *British Journal of Sociology of Education, 23,* (2), 210–232.

Sibley, D. (1995). *Geographies of exclusion: Society and difference in the West.* Routledge: New York.

Simmons, R. (2008). Raising the age of compulsory education in England: A NEET solution? *British Journal of Educational Studies*, 56, (4), 420–439.

Skeggs, B. (1997). *Formations of class and gender*. London: Sage.

Skeggs, B. (2004). *Class, self, culture*. London: Routledge.

Small, J. (1998). Ethnic and racial identity in adoption within the UK. In M. Hill, & M. Shaw (Eds.), *Signposts in adoption: Policy, practice and research issues* (pp. 191–205). London: BAAF.

Smith, H. Y. (1996). Building on the strengths of black families: Self-help and empowerment. In S. L. Logan (Ed.), *The black family: Strengths, self-help and positive change* (pp. 21–38). Boulder, CO: Westview Press.

Smith, R. (1998). *No lessons learnt*. London: The Children's Society.

Social Exclusion Unit (1999a). *Bridging the gap: New opportunities for 16–19 year olds not in education, employment or training*. London: The Stationery Office.

Social Exclusion Unit (1999b). *Truancy and school exclusion*. London: The Stationery Office.

Spicker, P. (1984). *Stigma and social welfare*. London: Palgrave Macmillan.

Stephen, D., & Squires, P. (2003). Adults don't realise how sheltered they are: A contribution to the debate on youth transitions from some voices on the margins. *Journal of Youth Studies*, 6, (2), 145–164.

Sudarkasa, N. (1997). African American families and family values. In H. P. McAdoo (Ed.), *Black families* (pp. 9–40). London: Sage.

Taylor, M. (1981). *Caught between: a review of research into the education of pupils of West Indian origin*. Windsor: NFER-Nelson.

Thernstrom, A., & Thernstrom, S. (2003). *No more excuses: Closing the racial gap in learning*. New York: Simon & Schuster.

Thomas, R., Henderson, S., & Holland, L. (2003). Making the most of what you've got? Resources, values and inequalities in young women's transitions to adulthood. *Educational Review*, 55, (1), 33–46.

Thomson, R., Bell, R., Holland, J., Henderson, S., McGrellis, S., & Sharpe, S. (2002). Critical moments: Choice, chance and opportunity in young people's narratives of transition. *Sociology*, 36, 335–354.

Tomlinson, S. (2008). *Race and education: Policy and politics in Britain*. Maidenhead: Open University Press/McGraw-Hill Education.

Toynbee, P., & Walker, D. (2008). *Unjust rewards: Exposing greed and inequality in Britain today*. London: Granta Publications.

Troyna, B. (1984). Fact or artefact? The educational underachievement of black pupils. *British Journal of Sociology of Education*, 5, (2), 158–160.

U.S. Department of Education (2002). *No child left behind*. Washington: DOE.

Wallman, S. (Ed.) (1979). *Ethnicity at work*. London: Macmillan.

Weekes, D., & Wright, C. (1998). *Improving practice, a whole school approach to raising the achievement of African Caribbean youth*. London: Nottingham Trent University/The Runnymede Trust.

West, C. (1995). Foreword. In K. Crenshaw, N. Gotanda, G. Peller, & K. Thomas (Eds.), *Critical race theory: The key writings that formed the movement* (pp. 62–72). New York: New Press.

Wetherell, M., Lafleche, M., Berkeley, R. (2007). *Identity, ethnic diversity and community cohesion.* London: Sage.

Williams, P. (2002). Individual agency and the experience of New Deal. *Journal of Education and Work, 15,* (1), 53–74.

Willis, P. (1977). *Learning to labour.* Farnborough: Saxon House.

Wilson, W. J. (1987). *The truly disadvantaged: The inner city, the underclass, and public policy.* Chicago: University of Chicago Press.

Wright, C. (1987). Black students – white teachers. In B. Troyna (Ed.), *Racial inequality in education* (pp. 109–126). London: Allen and Unwin.

Wright, C., Standen, P., John, G., German, G., & Patel, T. (2005). *Overcoming school exclusion and achieving successful youth transitions within African Caribbean communities.* York: Joseph Rowntree Foundation.

Wright, C., Weekes, D., & McGlaughlin, A. (2000). *'Race', class and gender in exclusion from school.* London: RoutledgeFalmer.

Wright, C., Weekes, D., McGlaughlin, A., & Webb, D. (1998). Masculinised discourses within education and the construction of black male identities amongst African-Caribbean youth. *British Journal of Sociology of Education, 19,* (1), 75–87.

Wyn, J., & White, R. (1998). Young people, social problems and Australian youth studies. *Journal of Youth Studies, 1,* (1), 23 –38.

Yosso, T. J. (2005). Whose culture has capital? A critical race theory discussion of community cultural wealth. *Race, Ethnicity and Education, 8,* (1), 69–91.

Youdell, D. (2003). Identity traps, or how black students fail. *British Journal of Sociology of Education, 24,* (1), 3–30.

Zirkel, S., & Cantor, N. (2004). 50 years after Brown v Board of education: The promise and challenge of multicultural education. *Journal of Social Issues, 60,* (1), 1–16.

Index